# JESUS B.

The Calling of Every Christian

JIM LYON

## Warner Press

Anderson, Indiana

Published by Warner Press Inc.
Warner Press and the "WP" logo are trademarks of Warner Press Inc.

Warner Press, Inc.
PO Box 2499
Anderson, IN 46018-2499
800-741-7721
www.warnerpress.org

Library of Congress Cataloging-in-Publication Data

Lyon, Jim (Pastor)
  Jesus B. : the calling of every Christian / Jim Lyon.
     pages cm
  Includes bibliographical references and index.
   ISBN 978-1-59317-680-8 (pbk. : alk. paper) -- ISBN 978-1-59317-681-5 (ebook : alk. paper)
  1. Christian life. 2. Identification (Religion)  I. Title.
   BV4501.3.L96 2015
   248.4--dc23
                              2015013292

ISBN: 978-1-59317-680-8

Printed in the United States of America.

# TABLE OF CONTENTS

# INTRODUCTION

Sometimes the obvious is the most profound, the elementary the most advanced. Sometimes we pass by transformational truth, plainly stated on the page, because it has been read so often it's dulled by its familiarity. We use words and phrases glibly in the world of faith, without pausing to comprehend the simple power of hearing them for the first time.

*The body of Christ.* Is it possible that we actually are the hands and feet of Christ? Here? Now? *The mind of Christ.* Is it possible that we can actually think and perceive, conceive and act as Jesus did and does? *I have given you an example to follow. Do as I have done to you.* These are the words of Jesus. Is it actually possible to be like Jesus? To Jesus be?

*Jesus B.* Yes, it sounds at once pretentious and contrived when rolled off the tongue. And yet, it is a thoughtful invitation—and a challenge—to dive deeper into the Christian life by taking the words and phrases of Scripture at face value, simply, purely, deeply. It is not a cheesy play on words; it is a serious shorthand that, in a way, captures the calling of every Christian.

The book that follows was born in a sermon series: seven weeks exploring the dare to Jesus B. delivered in the context of a local church's weekly worship service. The chapters are transcripts of teaching delivered originally from a platform to as fine a congregation of Jesus-followers as could be found anywhere.

A pastor, teaching week-by-week, is framed by the realization that his or her audience is not monolithic. Some in the audience are regulars, who have listened to more sermons and expositions of Scripture than they can remember. Others are seeking answers and appear on a Sunday for the single purpose of finding one. Still others will be present not by custom or by spiritual thirst, but under duress (family pressures to show up, for instance) or curiosity, skeptics prone to find fault or oblivious to the Spirit of the meeting. Others will listen on a spectrum encompassing everything in between. Each of these audiences must be addressed; each must find something of use; each must be drawn closer into the will and way of our Maker, for having heard the Word. This, at least, has been this pastor's ambition, week-by-week, in content and delivery.

Hearing the Jesus B. teaching series does not have quite the same effect as reading it. The spoken word naturally employs some connecting words, punctuation, and repetition for impact that are not necessary in print. The passing moment of audible speech requires, at times, a different tack than ideas captured on a page that can be studied. Nevertheless, the best communicators speak as they write and write as they speak; this, too, has been my ambition. Consequently, the reader of this collection of sermons will find ideas projected in the moment from a platform not always perfectly crafted for print but, perhaps in this case, arresting for their immediacy. The reader, hopefully, will also appreciate the attempt to address an audience at different points in a spiritual continuum with content designed for all, not just a niche.

It is a sobering exercise to stand and speak with Jesus as the subject. It is a serious business to teach and preach—and then to practice what you preach and teach day-by-day. It is a sacred privilege to speak into another's life. As I have reviewed the transcripts of the messages captured in this book, I have been reminded of all these things. And my prayer for all who read this book is the same as it was for the church family that was my original audience: that you will grow more like Christ for having been exposed to these ideas.

Jesus is the subject. He is the first and the last, the beginning and the end, the exact representation of God in human form, the Savior, friend, and the Lord of all. As Jesus is the subject, we are called by His hand and Spirit to be verbs, action words in real life, real time. *Jesus B.* And be encouraged.

Jim Lyon

# 1. WHO DO YOU WANT TO BE?

Have you ever been asked, "What do you want to be when you grow up?" Another way of asking the question is: "Who do you want to be?" Not just *what*, but *who*. The difference is significant, because *what* refers to your vocation, while *who* refers your identity or character.

When I was a young boy, I wanted to be a train engineer. Growing up in Seattle, my mom would often take me to Carkeek Park, a breathtaking wooded ravine hard and fast against the city's northwest shoreline. At the park's edge, where woods meet the pebbled shore of Puget Sound, there is a train track, hugging the foot of a steep bluff for miles in both directions. Every now and then, while exploring the rocks and sand of the beach at Carkeek, where Piper's Creek pours into the Sound, a train would blow its horn and rumble by. The ground trembled; the noise could be deafening; the power of the engine and the cars it pulled was mesmerizing as the salt-water surf crashed against the rail bed. I could never take my eyes off the train as it moved along its serpentine path from North Beach to Richmond Beach, dreaming of the day when I might be the engineer. I wanted to be the engineer. I played with wooden and electric trains at home; I built bridges, carved train track beds in the dirt of my backyard; I watched a local afternoon children's program after school every day: "Brakeman Bill." I was all about trains, until I became a teenager and realized

I was less-than-mechanically inclined and, well, not very engineer-like.

My dad once took me to the home of a dentist friend on Mercer Island, a tony, upscale island enclave set in the deep blue waters of Lake Washington, which defines Seattle's eastern boundary. I was fourteen and in ninth grade, and it was the most spectacular home I had ever seen. It had a cavernous foyer, with two sweeping staircases curved elegantly on either side, meeting to form one grand staircase beneath a towering window framing the evergreens outside. "If this is where dentists live," I thought, "then, *I want to be a dentist.*" But then I had my first real dental work done—not just a check-up, but a shot-in-the-gum line, drilling of the cavity-laden tooth, and filling of the damaged cuspid. Ouch. That dentist hurt me. Never mind that he was saving me from worse pain later; I knew then, staring into people's mouths, with needles and drills, day in and day out, would not be for me. *I can't do this! I can't hurt people for a living.* This episode (like others unmentioned) proved that this fourteen-year-old boy, like many others, was more informed by how things felt than thinking things through.

Next I dreamed of politics; I went so far as to imagine becoming president of the United States. It was preposterous then and seems absurd now, but I remember watching presidential candidates on television (Richard Nixon, Hubert Humphrey, Eugene McCarthy, George McGovern, and more) and thinking, *I could do that.*

In the end, I fell into the pastoral ministry. I say "fell into" it because that is how it felt to me. I did not choose it. I did not pursue it. I never imagined it, but I fell into it obediently when God opened the door.

It is sobering to look back over my life and consider why I am what I am. Subliminally, if not always consciously, I wrestled with the question many times: *what* do I want to be? I less often, but more deeply, also wrestled with the question: *who* do I want to be? Sometimes the questions seemed to be one;

at other times, they have stood separately. However, they are always connected.

The same is true for you. Your code of conduct, your dreams, your ambitions, your way of life, your value system, your goals, your relationships, everything that defines you is consequent to how, when, and whether you wrestle with these ultimate life questions. What do I want to do? And who do I want to be? Your answers will set you on a journey that lasts a lifetime.

## Who Wants to Be Like Jesus?

Most of us want to have a relationship with Jesus, but we're not so keen on being like Him. We want to have Jesus as our friend. We're fond of the sentiment of the song, "What a Friend We Have in Jesus." We want a supernatural companion who will come alongside us when we are in great difficulty, either because of our own poor choices or because of someone else's folly. There is no shame in saying, "I need God. I need to know that, when I must bear the unbearable, I am not alone."

Yes, most of us want to have a savior. We want to have a divine friend. But surrender our wills to Jesus Christ? Submit our life journey to His complete control? Take Jesus as the model for our lives? That can seem extreme.

There are a lot of things about Jesus that I would like to emulate. I'd like to be popular as He was, from time to time. I'd like to be able to work miracles. I'd like to be able to teach with the kind of authority that Jesus clearly demonstrated. I'd like to enjoy the wonderful, close friendships that Jesus seemed to have with those twelve guys He called the disciples.

But there's so much more about Jesus that I'm not sure I want to embrace. There's that whole poverty thing. You know, Jesus said, "I don't have anywhere to lay down my head" (Matt 8:20, para.). I'm certain I do not want to be single for my whole adult life, yet Jesus said I must be willing to forego such relationships to follow Him (see Matt 19:29). Though I sometimes feel victimized, I don't want to be a martyr in the way Jesus was (see Matt 24:9). I don't want to be Jesus in the storm; I don't want to be in the storm in the first place. I don't want to be Jesus rejected. I don't want to be Jesus alone. I don't want to be Jesus suffering, physically or emotionally or in any other way. I don't want to be clothed by pain, no matter how noble the cause. I don't want to be Jesus crying, "My God, my God! Why have you abandoned me?" (Matt 27:46). I don't want to be that kind of Jesus.

Yet, the truth is, if we are to experience the abundant life that Jesus promises, if we are in fact to walk with Him, we must be willing to accept the whole of Jesus' life, not just the parts that appeal to us.

In no way would I suggest that any of us could be the Savior. We cannot. Jesus alone was without fault and consequently the only one ever to live on this earth qualified to lay down His life on our behalf and carry our sins to the grave. He alone lived in this world without sin; He has no sin to carry to the cross—save our own. Only Jesus could be the Savior of the world. He's the only one who could be the Redeemer. None of us can redeem the souls of others in the way Jesus redeems. None of us can make others whole in the way Jesus can. None of us can be the Son of God in the way Jesus is the Son of God. Only He is the exact representation of God in human form. When we see Jesus, we see the Father. He is the word of God become flesh. He is the one mediator between heaven and earth. We cannot intercede for others in the same way He does. And yet...

We can be Jesus in more ways than we might imagine. I challenge you to consider how God might use you to be Jesus to someone else—and I challenge you to make yourself available for that purpose.

As I mentioned earlier, I don't want to be Jesus the Suffering Servant; I can't imagine enduring the torture His enemies inflicted upon Him. But I would be kidding myself if I thought that I could avoid suffering if I refused to follow Jesus. What nonsense. Everyone suffers. Suffering is a part of this broken world. We do not escape suffering if we refuse to be like Jesus; we simply suffer without the benefit of His wisdom and His power.

We're all going to stub our toes. We're all going to have broken bones and broken hearts. The question is not whether we will escape the shadows of our fallen world, but whether we will be able to rise above them.

*How do we overcome suffering?* When we frame the question in this way, being like Jesus is by far the best way to live. Nobody who has walked in this world has experienced its spiritual and emotional mountaintops more joyfully and perfectly than Jesus has experienced them. Nobody has been able to walk through "the darkest valley" (Ps 23:4) of this life and come out of it as well as Jesus has. If I want to live completely, if I want to live abundantly, if I want to be filled with life, if I want to be a person who adds to life and does not take away from life, then Jesus is the singular outstanding pioneer and model, the Master of Life. More than any other person, Jesus is the one person I want to be. Jesus B.

## The Believer's Shorthand

I realize that it sounds a bit like Yoda in a *Star Wars* film to put the verb at the end of a statement in this way, but I propose that "Jesus Be" become a kind of shorthand for any who follow Christ. We might use the abbreviation in two ways:

First, when we find ourselves tempted to do wrong, we can stop and say to ourselves, "Jesus B. I am going to face and resist temptation, as did Jesus, instead of going my old way into the arms of temptation." If you see me faltering or being less faithful than Jesus would have been, I hope you will say to me with a kind, gentle smile, "Jim, Jesus B. Be like Jesus right now." Just by hearing it, I'll be brought back to the reality of my commitments and my call. In the same way, I hope you will allow me to say when you are wavering in your commitment to Christ, "George, Sally…Jesus B. Jesus B."

Second, we can speak this as a word of encouragement. In moments when we become channels of God's mercy, grace, and forgiveness, how sweet it would be for someone to say to us, "Thanks be to God. I see Jesus in you." What a wonderful— the most profound—compliment. What extraordinary praise. We always think about praising people for the way they look or what they've acquired or their talents or skill sets, but imagine being so sensitive to the Spirit of the living God in one another that in those small yet eternal moments of kindness and grace, we would say, "Oh, it's so good to be with you. Jesus B."

I want to be like Jesus; I know this is a tall order. It is scary even to say such a thing, but I think God is calling every Christian to this most empowering of ambitions. If we are to be the body of Christ, we have to Jesus B. If we're to have the mind of Christ, to perceive our world with all of its opportunities and challenges as Jesus does, we must Jesus B. If we're going to follow Jesus in full obedience, we have to Jesus B. If we're going to walk through this world with the attitudes of Jesus, we have to Jesus B. If we are to forgive others freely and know the wholeness of receiving forgiveness from heaven, we'll have to Jesus B. Truth be told, unless we become like Jesus, we'll never fulfill our calling to be His disciples. We'll never even come close. But as the Spirit of the living Christ possesses us, we can become like Jesus day by day, more and more, until at the last we are received into His arms, hearing, "Well done, my good and faithful servant" (Matt 25:21).

I received my bachelor's degree from Seattle Pacific University. As a student resident on campus, I lived on the fifth floor of Ashton Hall. One of the guys in my class, named Chris, lived down the hall from me. Chris had, shall we say, the gift of song. Morning, noon, and night. He was a fine musician, both a vocalist and instrumentalist, and he composed tunes, too. He was also a leader and was forever seeking ways to corral all of us into singing together.

There were about fifty young men on the floor. Chris pulled us together in the dorm lounge, perched on the fifth floor Ashton ledge. Ashton Hall was built into a steep incline of Queen Anne Hill's north slope, overlooking the Lake Washington Ship Canal and the sharp rise of Seattle's Phinney Ridge beyond. Crowded into the lounge and spilling out through the floor-to-ceiling glass of the adjacent balcony, the fifth floor guys listened and learned as Chris played his guitar and directed what the campus would eventually dub, "the Fifth Floor Ashton SuperChoir." These were the days of Simon and Garfunkel, Phoebe Snow, and pop-folk secular culture. The "SuperChoir" would sing at random (albeit rarely) around the campus and, once, even in the campus chapel services. Our signature piece was a song that Chris wrote, capturing Philippians 1:6 (in the then newly released New American Standard Bible): "I am confident of this very thing, that He who began the good work in you will perfect it until the day of Christ Jesus."

Think of it: God Himself discipling us. If God begins a good work in you (as the Holy Spirit draws you to Christ), then He will perfect that work (by the transformational power and equipping of His Spirit, making you more and more like Jesus). As we are perfected, He is glorified; the world can look at our lives and recognize His signature. As the world looks at us and says, "Jesus B.," we become evidence of the Scripture brought to life.

How does this journey begin? Let's see how it began for Jesus.

## Jesus' Public Commitment

Jesus' cousin John had become a phenomenon. Thousands upon thousands streamed into the wilderness of Judea to see this preacher who ate bizarre natural foods and dressed in an avant-garde manner—wearing a loin cloth of animal skin. Jesus went to where John was preaching and the crowds were gathering. Here's how Matthew 3 describes it:

> Jesus went from Galilee to the Jordan River to be baptized by John. But John tried to talk him out of it. "I am the one who needs to be baptized by you," he said, "so why are you coming to me?" But Jesus said, "It should be done for we must carry out all that God requires." So John agreed to baptize him. After his baptism, as Jesus came up out of the water, the heavens were opened and he saw the Spirit of God descending like a dove and settling on him. A voice from heaven said, "This is my dearly loved Son who brings me great joy." (vv 13–17)

The New Testament tells us a good deal about the birth of Jesus and one brief incident from His boyhood, but we have a huge gap in the Gospel narrative from that incident (when Jesus was 12-years-old) until He burst forth on the public stage. In the intervening years, we must assume that He had been getting ready for His ministry. He had been "waiting in the wings," so to speak. Now in Matthew 3, the hour had struck and Jesus walked onto the world stage; the first thing He did was present Himself to be baptized.

I believe that if you want to Jesus B., you must have a definite beginning of your own spiritual journey. By that I mean you must reach a point of decision about who you are and who you're going to be. All of us need to do that. Some people are raised in Christian homes and have been immersed in the knowledge of Scripture throughout childhood and adolescence. Many of these people cannot pinpoint a definitive moment when they surrendered their lives into God's hand. They say it just seemed to "evolve." I respect this kind of testimony. I know it is legitimate. In fact, you may have a story like that. But I'm here to tell you that if you want to Jesus B., you need to have a moment that is your public "coming out party." You need a day on which you step out of the background, stand forward, and make an irrevocable, cannot-be-misunderstood statement of who you are. That's what happened at the Jordan River. Jesus stepped forward in the most public way and declared His commitment to be God's man.

Some of us fear publicity. We shrink from the eye of public attention and say, "Make a public declaration? That's just not for me." But there must be one moment where you stand in the spotlight of heaven so the whole world can see who you are. There has to be a moment when all of hell knows the choice you have made. That moment is your baptism. It is when you say with Jesus, "This is who I am, and this is the path I will follow. Jesus is Lord, and I will serve Him. I admit my sin and have been cleansed from it by the blood of Christ, shed on the cross. My old life is dead and buried, and I have been raised to new life in Christ." It is all there in baptism. There can be no mistaking it. There will not be any question marks. There will not be any shadows. There will not be any wondering. When I go to my grave, people will be able to trace my journey back to the moment when I stood up and said, "I belong to God."

I became a Christian when I came forward to kneel before God at the end of a church meeting many years ago. I was just twelve years old, but it is a very vivid memory. That was the moment of my decision, and my public declaration of that decision—my baptism—soon followed. That was the sequence of events modeled for us by Jesus in His own baptism.

There's no way around it. Baptism needs to be elevated in the life of the church. It must be esteemed. It's not incidental or optional.

In preaching his first sermon on the Day of Pentecost, the apostle Peter said, "Repent and..." what? "Be baptized in the name of Jesus Christ for the forgiveness of your sins" (Acts 2:38). Baptism is an essential first step in a life of Christian discipleship. I would no more encourage you to begin a journey with

God without baptism than I would encourage you to begin a marriage relationship without a wedding ceremony. It is the public manifestation of your intention. Jesus stood forward in a very public way, in the most public forum of His time, and asked John to baptize Him. John was reluctant because he knew who Jesus was, but Jesus said, "It should be done, for we must carry out all that God requires" (Matt 3:15). Jesus had no sin from which He could repent. He had no flaw to be mended. He did not need to state that He was going to begin obeying God. (He was God.) But He wanted to model for us this signal of the New Testament age, this marker that for 20 centuries has separated those who follow Jesus from those who do not. He said, "I will be baptized. John, you must do it. It is required." And so it is for everyone who wants to Jesus B.

### The First Step of Obedience: Baptism

I do not believe that baptism is the gateway to salvation or that it somehow seals us for salvation. We are saved by faith, and saving faith is our acceptance, in the deepest part of our being, of the Savior whose death on the cross saves us. However, we must not let that vital truth obscure another very important truth: *Faith that is not demonstrated is not faith at all.* If you're not obedient even in the most elemental parts of the gospel call, how can you have faith enough to carry you forward into eternity? John and Peter said, "Repent and be baptized." That is the sequence of events—repent (turn away from your sin) and then be baptized (demonstrate publicly that you intend to leave sin behind). Jesus had nothing for which to repent, so He went straight to baptism. If you want to be Jesus, you will have to be baptized, too. If you've been a believer for thirty years and have not been baptized, now is the time. If you came to Jesus last year and you haven't followed Him in baptism, now is the time. If you think you're going to follow Jesus but ignore the call to be baptized, you are already fumbling the ball. It is a singular act of obedience to the gospel. A life-changing relationship with God always hinges on obedience. To be obedient in baptism is essential to following Jesus.

You will find some strong differences of opinion among Christians about the correct manner of baptism—should we be baptized by immersion or by sprinkling? Should we be immersed just once or three times to recognize the three persons of the Trinity? Should infants be baptized or only adults? Such questions have circulated in the church for centuries.

For example, as Christianity entered northern Europe, where the weather could get very cold for much of the year, baptism became a sprinkling ritual in many communities. Since we now live in an age when it is possible to be baptized in warm water all year round, why not be immersed as Jesus was? There is important symbolism in immersion as well. When we are baptized, we, in a representational way, demonstrate that we are dead to sin, buried in Christ, and then raised up to new life in Him. Scripture tells us that the baptismal water represents God's cleansing of our sin. The water itself doesn't cleanse our sin, but it demonstrates that God does.

Religious rituals can do this—in a world where people cannot always read and do not always understand a theological vocabulary, these visual demonstrations of eternal truth are irreplaceable and unmistakable.

Another important truth is best depicted by being immersed in water: baptism declares that you submit yourself to God. When you are baptized by immersion, you must surrender control of your body, if but for a moment, to someone else's arms. You have to let that person take you under the water and raise you out of it again, and for some this is no small thing. I'll never forget the first baptism at which I officiated in Seattle. A friend named Polly DeGard had become a believer and wanted me to baptize her. Just before we stepped into the baptismal water, she said, "Jim, are you nervous? It's your first baptism." "Polly, why should I be nervous?" I asked. "I'm putting *you* under the water. Why aren't *you* nervous?" I have baptized many people since then, and the act itself has a special sacredness for me. Someone being baptized is completely helpless, off balance, and dependent on someone else. There's a powerful truth in that.

✳As you can tell, I favor baptism by immersion, but the manner of baptism is not a hobbyhorse for me. Don't let disputes about the manner of baptism distract you from the fact that you ought to be baptized. Baptism was a landmark event in the life of Jesus, and it will be the same for you.

Don't you think there was a hush in the air when John the Baptist, who'd been preaching so long about someone coming who was greater than he, finally announced that He had arrived? They heard John say, "No, no. I'm not worthy to baptize you." And they heard Jesus say, "You must. It is required."

Don't you imagine that the crowd gasped as Jesus of Nazareth went down into the water and came back up? There seemed to be a gasp in heaven because, at the baptism of Jesus, heaven opened. The barrier that ordinarily separates us from the supernatural of the unseen realm opened! For a brief shining moment, the Holy Spirit was palpable in the presence of a dove, and the voice of God spoke through heaven's window: "This is my Son. He pleases me greatly."

✳Your baptism can have its own marks of the supernatural. Your crowd of witnesses may not see heaven open. They may not hear the voice of God. But I believe that when you step forward in humble faith to be baptized, heaven does open. There's a turn of the knob and the door to eternity opens when you take that obedient step of public faith because God is very pleased by your obedience; it is the first step proving your love. I'll go so far as to say that the Holy Spirit hovers over you in baptism. Receiving the Holy Spirit always hinges on obedience, and few things could be more obedient than to be submerged in baptism for Jesus' sake.

What do you want to do? Who do you want to be? Jesus B.

# 2. JESUS B. SPIRIT-FILLED

If you would Jesus B., you should not only be baptized, but you must also come to terms with the new identity as His disciple that baptism proclaims. And then what? What happens then? Jesus' life took an unexpected turn after His own baptism, and we read about it in Matthew 4:

*Then Jesus was led by the Spirit into the wilderness to be tempted there by the devil. For forty days and forty nights he fasted and became very hungry. During that time the Devil came and said to him, "If you are the Son of God, tell these stones to become loaves of bread." But Jesus told him, "No! The Scriptures say,*

> *'People do not live by bread alone, but by every word that comes from the mouth of God.'"*

*Then the Devil took him to the holy city, Jerusalem, to the highest point of the Temple, and said, "If you are the Son of God, jump off! For the Scriptures say,*

> *'He will order his angels to protect you.*
> *And they will hold you up with their hands*
> *so you won't even hurt your foot on a stone.'"*
> *Jesus responded, "The Scriptures also say,*
> *'You must not test the LORD your God.'"*

*Next the Devil took him to the peak of a very high mountain and showed him all the kingdoms of the world and their glory. "I will give it all to you," he said, "if you will kneel down and worship me." "Get out of here, Satan," Jesus told him. "For the Scriptures say,*

> *'You must worship the LORD your God and serve only him.'"*

*Then the devil went away, and angels came and took care of Jesus. (vv 1-11)*

When we declare our fidelity to Jesus, we can be certain that the Devil himself will be lurking in the shadows to deter us, distract us, and, if possible, detour us from that straight and narrow way. So it was for our Lord. If Jesus himself was tempted, we will certainly be. In fact, did you notice in the text that Jesus was led "by the Spirit" into the wilderness, where He was tempted by the Devil? He was tempted by the Devil while following the very Holy Spirit that authenticated His witness at His baptism.

Temptation is an ordinary part of human life and experience. If we will Jesus B., we must come to grips with temptation and overcome it. Jesus faced temptation and was victorious over it. If we are to be like Him, we should have victory over temptation, too.

## Going a Different Way

The whole predicate of the Christian walk is that we can be transformed and made new so we can walk differently in the future than we have walked in the past. To repent and be baptized means to turn away from our native predisposition to sin, to moral failure, to being less than God created us to be. It is the chance to be free—to change course, to change direction, to be different than before. You cannot be baptized and, with integrity, continue living as you did before. Life in Christ is a new life, an abundant life.

The Devil will work tirelessly to prove this proposition false. He will use everything at his disposal to cause you to believe that you are still enslaved to him. He will try to tell you that you cannot overcome his beguiling ways. He whispered into the very heart of Jesus. Let's make this clear: the Devil talks. He speaks persuasively to the human heart. He speaks to unbelievers and to believers. He'll speak to the redeemed and those who are not yet redeemed. If he spoke into the heart and mind of Jesus, he can speak into our hearts and minds as well. Sometimes Satan speaks aloud, his temptation articulated by another voice in your world. Maybe he is speaking to you on the television, on the Internet, through your closest friends, through your co-workers. Even when he speaks without an audible sound, he can plant in your mind an idea that is designed to deceive you.

The Devil is the antithesis of truth. He is the opposite of what is right. He has no desire to work for your good, but seeks only your destruction. He feeds off your misery. Every idea that he plants in your heart and mind is crafted to subtract from, not add to, your life. To be able to persuade you to go his way, he must deceive you. No person would willingly walk into oblivion. None of us would consciously choose to harm ourselves, unless we were deceived into doing so. The enemy of our souls must use a mask, veil, or blinder to persuade us before we would ever do what he suggests. Consequently, his word is always false, clothed sometimes with half-truths, but fundamentally a lie. Most of us can differentiate between a bald-faced lie and the truth, so the Devil does not often traffic in the obvious lie. He prefers to speak deceptively in half-truths.

Did you notice in Matthew's account that the Devil actually quotes Scripture to Jesus? He attempts to persuade Jesus to do wrong by using the Word of God. Likewise, in our day the Scripture can be turned on its head. It can be quoted out of context. It can be spun in ways that appeal to our own egos, our own pride, our own selfishness, our own preferences, or our own hearts' desire. Satan can point to Scripture to rationalize the way we think things should be. He can interpret Scripture in ways that are actually oppositional to what God intended. Beware—it is not enough just to have a biblical passage that seems to support a certain course of action. It is not enough to think, *This makes sense to me.* The question should always be: what is God's truth in not just the passage but in the sum of Scripture? Who and what would Jesus B.?

## Temptation #1: Providing for Yourself

The Devil approached Jesus with a series of temptations. Notice their progression. The first temptation is quite ordinary. It deals with a basic human need; Jesus is hungry. He is fasting as He pursues God. The Son of God incarnate is working toward a deeper union with His Father in heaven. To this end, He denies His flesh in a forty-day fast. Still His body cries out in hunger. Bread please. There's no shame in wanting bread, is there?

I'm a bread fancier myself. You know what I really like? Sourdough bread—sourdough on the West Coast, sourdough born in San Francisco, sourdough heavy and textured. This kind of sourdough so prevalent on the West Coast was a staple of my childhood. Unrestrained, I would toast half a loaf of sourdough bread—not too dark, just enough to be crunchy—and melt butter on it until it glistened in the sunshine. The other half of the loaf I would eat untoasted and slathered with butter, so thick that I could feel the cool, hard butter cut by my teeth with every bite. Mouthwateringly delicious? Absolutely. Healthy? Not so much, but still with some nutrients and benefit. There are times when I crave that bread, not because I've been on a forty-day fast, but just because I desire it, I am hungry for it. Bread can be a fit emblem of many things that are not necessarily bad for us. Bread itself does little harm if eaten in moderation, yet even something this good for us can lure us into gluttony. Things that we think are just the stuff of ordinary daily life can claim too large a place in our hearts and distract us from what is more important.

The Devil encouraged Jesus to turn rocks into bread. "Just use Your supernatural power, Jesus. What's the big deal? You're hungry!" Jesus was on a journey to see God, and the Devil urged him to see dinner. Jesus was trying to hear from heaven, and the Devil tried to get Jesus' stomach to growl so loudly that He could hear nothing else. So it will be in our lives. Whether it is food for your body, a relationship that normally would be healthy—whatever it might be—if you allow something good to take priority over your pursuit of God, it can lead you to ruin.

The temptation to make bread was not bizarre or outrageous. This temptation involved crossing a line to grasp the ordinary. We are so steeled against things that we might obviously perceive as sinful that the Devil will weave temptation into the otherwise mundane. If you want to Jesus B., you must submit to Him even the routine things of life. Day by day, you must be ready to say, "I am seeking God—even if it means I don't eat bread today."

## Temptation #2: Acting on Impulse

The next temptation involved an appeal to pleasure, to thrilling experience, to excitement. The Devil took Jesus up to the temple. Did Jesus actually find himself standing physically on the pinnacle of the temple? Perhaps, but I am not sure. I wonder if this whole scenario took place in the Lord's extraordinary ability to see and know beyond the material reality of the moment—very real temptations, to be sure, but perhaps in ways we cannot presently understand. However it was, Jesus saw Himself at a high place and heard Satan say, "Throw Yourself off. Think what it would be like. Think about the rush, the wind against your face, and the experience of freedom. Jump out! Fall into the arms of God; He'll take care of you! He'll protect You. His love, His care trumps everything else, doesn't it? Even Your own folly."

Perhaps, this temptation was also an appeal to public pride. "Go ahead, create a spectacle, and watch how the crowds watch You with awe and amazement. Why wait to work miracles on the street when You can grab the headlines with Your own death-defying tricks now?"

I have never been taken to the top of a high building and prompted to jump off, but I've been on many precipices in my life where the Devil whispered in my ear, "Jim, just go for it. God loves you. His hand is on you; He has great plans for you. Don't worry! Just go for it! Do what you will." The Devil is always pushing people to suspend their own good judgment, their sense of consequence, and go for it.

### Temptation #3: Switching Loyalties

Then Jesus is confronted by a temptation more profound. The Devil shows Him all the kingdoms of the world and says, "All Yours. It's all Yours. Just worship me. Just suspend this silly devotion to a God in heaven. Look at the tangible realities of the world instead. See with your eyes, touch with your hands, smell with your nostrils, taste with your mouth. Look at it all! It's all Yours. The only thing You must do is abandon that devotion to God and worship me. Give yourself to me; I'll make it all Yours."

I travel to India often. The subcontinent captured my heart when I first visited in 1987 and has held me ever since. I am no stranger to Hindu temples; I believe that it was important for me to visit some to comprehend the spiritual frame of the hundreds of millions of Hindu Indians who revere them. Photography is generally forbidden inside the temples, but each temple has essentially the same floor plan and blueprint (although they can vary widely in size). There's usually a principal deity (sometimes two) in the center courtyard, at the heart of the temple, a kind of holy of holies. There's an outer second courtyard and a third peripheral courtyard. As you go deeper into the temple compound, you may pass many subordinate deities, often lesser gods in relationship to the idol at the center.

Once, while in a remote town in Tamil Nadu in the south of India, where westerners rarely travel, a Brahmin priest escorted me through the temple in which he served. He was very proud to introduce me to what was, for him, primary, beautiful, powerful, and transcendent. I asked him, "What do you believe these gods do for you?"

He replied, gesturing, his face serious, focused, "This god is for a crop of corn. This god will help you with your rice crop. This god will help you with your cattle. This god will help you with your wife." There was a god for everything you can imagine in ordinary life in south India. Suddenly, my guide stopped and said, "Now look at this god." I stared at the stone figure for a moment at which he pointed; then the priest literally whispered in my ear, "This god will fulfill your wildest dreams. Anything you could possibly imagine, anything you could want. Anything you could desire, this god will fulfill. *Just worship him.*" He whispered breathlessly, in a low, deliberate tone.

I was strangely drawn in. I must confess I began to toy with his suggestive thoughts, imagining things I wanted but did not have, experiences of which I had dreamed but never realized, shadows dredged from desire fostered not by heaven but by hell. Without warning, I was no longer thinking about the ridiculous proposition that a rock carved with human hands had divine life and was a god, but instead I found my mind racing into all kinds of places it had never gone before. It was very attractive, it was very compelling, it was very persuasive, magnetic in a way. Then, by the grace of God, the Holy Spirit spoke into my heart and said, "Jim Lyon, get out of here *now.*"

"You'll have to excuse me, but I'm leaving," I told the priest, as he still whispered seductively into my ear. He seemed surprised.

"Oh, no! Please, come back. Look—stare—at the god some more."

"No, I'm done." I walked straight out the door. When I got outside I took a deep breath and realized how close I had come. Temptation, spiritual entrapment, and the contest for our heart's allegiance are real. It was palpable that day.

The Devil will try everything in his power to tempt you. How do you Jesus B. when he determinedly does? You and I will face temptations until the last day, until that day when the Lord vanquishes Satan forever.

Here's what Jesus did. First, He chose to be God's. He made a decision about who and what He would be. "I have come down from heaven to do the will of God who sent me" (John 6:38). You must make this your overriding ambition as well. It is a choice that each of us can only make for ourselves. If that ambition is compromised by anything else, you will not Jesus B. I do not know what life trajectory the Lord has for you; I cannot tell what vocation He has providentially appointed for you; I cannot tell you definitely about your ministry. But I can tell you that God has a plan and path—a will—for your life. Are you absolutely committed to the fulfillment of His will—at the expense of your own preferences, your own desires, your own template for the way you think things should be? Could you choose to serve God above all other things? If so, are you willing to immerse yourself in the Scriptures?

You see, Jesus refuted the Devil with Scripture. He quoted Scripture three times, in three temptations, all from the book of Deuteronomy. (In fact, you may want to study Deuteronomy; it seemed to serve Jesus well.) You need to be a student of the Word. You need to integrate the Word into the very fiber of your being. You need to memorize Scripture like you memorize phone numbers and stats about quarterbacks. Apply that same focused mental preoccupation to God's Word. Then when temptation comes, God will bring to mind the Scripture with which to refute and stand down the Enemy.

Finally, you must also be led by the Spirit. Remember how the Holy Spirit descended upon Jesus as He was baptized? The heavens opened, and the Spirit appeared in the form of a dove. "This is my dearly loved Son, who brings me great joy," God said (Matt 3:17). The Spirit then led Jesus into this place of testing. Note that the Spirit will never lead you into temptation that you cannot bear. If the Holy Spirit possesses you, the Spirit will give you power to defeat the tempter and live above that sin. It is not sin to be tempted. It is sin to allow your mind to embrace its outcome. You cannot resist it unless you are surrendered into the Holy Spirit, until the Holy Spirit is an active, resident part of your daily life and journey. The Holy Spirit can empower you; the Holy Spirit will remind you of the teaching, the words, and the thoughts of Jesus. The Holy Spirit can speak into your heart and mind. The Holy Spirit will call you out of the danger zone. The Holy Spirit will draw the boundaries, but you must be surrendered to Him.

The Holy Spirit is not just some kind of theological principle, an ephemeral premise, or an esoteric concept or force. He is a living reality, a Persona of the one God of heaven and earth who equips, protects, and seals us for the last day. Are you surrendered into that Spirit?

Are you allowing yourself to be possessed by the Holy Spirit? If you stumble, each time you sin, every time you chose to fail, you create a barrier with God. The free flow of the Spirit's power cannot be then restored until that sin is repented and confessed. Live in a way that the Spirit has freedom to operate within you. The more that the Spirit has that freedom, the more spiritual power will come your way, and the more you will Jesus B. as His Spirit works within you.

You can be baptized. You can make the decision you want to Jesus B. But these alone will not be enough to realize your hope. You must also open your heart and mind, unreservedly, to the setting apart, the possession, and the supernatural agency of the Holy Spirit. Bow before Him and ask to be filled as you pledge to surrender to the One whose love for you knows no limit.

# 3. JESUS B. THE LIGHT

When I was a student in Seattle Public Schools, American presidents were presented altogether as heroic figures, icons of virtue, courage, and goodness. Rarely did we read or hear anything to the contrary. The presidents of history (and at the time) seemed to walk on higher ground, even as their modest roots and "common man" biographies inspired their journeys. That was the way American history was understood.

In the present day, textbooks have shown us that presidents, too, can have feet of clay. We've learned some things about some who have lived in the White House that do not inspire, that are less than noble. An aggressive press, the scrub of history, the glare of cameras, and the unrelenting stalking of social media have opened doors that could not have even been imagined at Webster Elementary School perched on Seattle's Sunset Hill. We've now seen leaders in the Oval Office through the lens of both strengths and weaknesses, some more than others.

I am not persuaded that presidents are of lesser caliber these days; I suspect we are just more honest about them. Of course, the shifting and increasing relativism framing the culture's moral sense is reflected in the halls of government too. (Our leaders often do not lead so much as they reflect public attitudes. Can we reasonably expect those we choose to govern us to be morally more than we are?) At any rate, presidential foibles and personal failures are not shielded in the way they have been in the past. We have become accustomed to seeing presidents as flawed by the fall, too.

Each one of us chooses somebody—maybe in politics, in sports, in the business world, in church leadership, or even in our immediate families—to serve as a model for our life's course. Subliminally or intentionally, we will become what we admire. That's just human nature. We survey the world as we know it and choose to become like so-and-so, consciously or unconsciously.

A great Church of God preacher named Gerald Marvel passed away a few years ago in Washington state. When I was a student at Warner Pacific College in Portland, Oregon, he served as senior pastor at Vancouver's First Church of God. His distinguished ministry there would span decades.

I'll never forget Gerald's preaching skill. He was a phenomenon, as gifted as any man or woman ever to stand behind a pulpit (or, in Gerald's case, without one). On the Warner Pacific campus, none of us had ever heard anything like it. Over the years, many Warner Pacific students destined for the pastoral ministry reached to imitate Gerald-on-the-platform. The simple stance, without lectern or notes, the flash of a grin, the stare at the floor while building a story, the reach of his arm and sweep of a gesture, the inescapable and persuasive charm of a certain common sense and logic, the grounding in the Word, these were the markers of greatness, so we believed. There was even a term for it: *Marvelesque*. We wanted to be *Marvelesque*, like Gerald Marvel.

I was a member of that Marvelesque generation. Many of us who imitated Gerald Marvel did not do so intentionally. We were so influenced by his presentation, which was uniformly effective, that we just naturally began to mimic what we saw, often without even trying to do so. Whatever our aspiration, we tend to replicate the veneer and sometimes the core of those who walk ahead of us, successfully. This is endemic in human nature.

And who will model his or her life after you? You are being watched today as surely as Gerald Marvel was watched on the Sunday platform of his congregation in Vancouver. Your audience may not be as large or varied, but you have an audience. Everyone does. It is likely, even though you may not see yourself as worth emulating, that you have several "someones" who are your understudies right now. What are you modeling for them? How are you preparing them for the stage of life?

## Ways We Can Jesus B.

Matthew's Gospel challenges us to Jesus B. Unlike all the figures of Hollywood, unlike all of the presidents of the United States, unlike all of the so-called greats in our world today, this one Man is perfect. This one Man has transcended time and space to influence in a constructive way more persons than anyone in all of history. This one Man lived more holistically, more fully, more richly, more deeply, more successfully than anyone else. He laughed authentically and wept unashamedly. He experienced the whole roller coaster of life's emotions and handled them skillfully, perfectly. Jesus. If we are going to aspire to be like someone, why not Jesus B.?

However, as I observed earlier, you cannot be the Redeemer of the world. You cannot be the Savior of humanity, as He is. You will never be morally perfect, which qualified Jesus to take our sin to the cross, satisfying the justice of the universe. You and I can never Jesus B. by these ultimate measures.

But we still can be salt and light as He was. We can express the heart of God in the gestures we make, in the words we speak, and in the ways we think. Yes, we can even have the mind of Christ, as the Scripture says. We can be transformed by the renewing of our minds. We can do marvelous things as Jesus did and even greater things. He promised this much to His disciples. Each of us can be a part of the living body of Christ. We can Jesus B. in our uniquely individual, albeit limited, ways.

We saw in the first chapter that if you want to Jesus B., you must be baptized. You must step forward in public and say, "This is who I am." When you obey God's call to baptism, you make that public statement of who you are. It is not enough to come forward at the end of a worship service and pray the sinner's prayer. It's not enough to pledge to make a new start with your life. It's not enough to write a letter to your grandmother promising to be better. You need to be baptized. Jesus was, and if Jesus needed to be obedient to his heavenly Father in this, what makes you think you do not? Baptism will not save you, but it is an important step if you want to Jesus B. in your world.

Second, you must open your heart to the power of the Holy Spirit so that you can have victory over temptation. The fourth chapter of Matthew describes the temptation of Jesus in the wilderness. It says that the power of the Holy Spirit, which led him into the desert, helped him overcome the tempter there. You must do the same. You are going to face temptation until your last breath. The Devil will be tireless in trying to detour you from the Way. He will try to wrench you from the grasp of God. He will try to convince you that you are not worthy and that your case is hopeless. He will try to insinuate that you cannot overcome his wily temptation. After all, you're "only human."

The Holy Spirit will contradict that voice. If you decide you want to Jesus B. and you surrender yourself to the governance of the Holy Spirit as He did, you can stare the devil down, too. Point by point, Jesus refuted the Devil's lies: "People do not live by bread alone" (Matt 4:4). "You must not test the Lord your God" (Matt 4:7). "Get out of here, Satan" (Matt 4:10). All of this was done in the power of the Holy Spirit, and that Spirit can help you Jesus B. today.

## Be God's Light

What's next? Scripture tells us that Jesus is light in Matthew 4. The verses below are seldom read together, but this passage reads as a seamless whole. It describes how Jesus comes up out of the wilderness after being tempted by Satan. He has had spiritual victory. Angels have ministered to Him. However, Jesus hears that King Herod has arrested John the Baptist, so He resolves to return to Galilee. Here is how the Bible describes it:

"In the land of Zebulun and of Naphtali,
  beside the sea, beyond the Jordan River,
  in Galilee where so many Gentiles live,
the people who sat in darkness
  have seen a great light.
And for those who lived in the land where death
casts its shadow,
  a light has shined."

31

From then on Jesus began to preach, "Repent of your sins and turn to God, for the Kingdom of Heaven is near."

One day as Jesus was walking along the shore of the Sea of Galilee, he saw two brothers—Simon, also called Peter, and Andrew—throwing a net into the water, for they fished for a living. Jesus called out to them, "Come, follow me, and I will show you how to fish for people!" And they left their nets at once and followed him.

A little farther up the shore he saw two other brothers, James and John, sitting in a boat with their father, Zebedee, repairing their nets. And he called them to come, too. They immediately followed him, leaving the boat and their father behind. (vv 15–22)

Zebulun and Naphtali were the names of two of the ancient tribes of Israel. When the Hebrews escaped from Egypt and its slavery and found their way at last to the Promised Land, these two tribes were assigned the northern tier of the territory of what would be called the land of Israel. Because they were on the northern border, they were generally the first to be attacked by marauders from other empires and neighboring countries. Over many centuries, Zebulun and Naphtali became regional names for the area in which these two tribes settled. It became suffering land, not only a place where people were often assaulted but also one where there was intermingling with pagan peoples and the watering down of God-given values. This region became, over centuries, a tumultuous cauldron of competing, merging, and contesting cultures and peoples.

It's very much the same today in the northern part of Israel. The villages, towns, and cities of Israel, which are up against the Lebanese and Syrian borders, are frequent targets of missile attacks and armed volleys from the other side. Because this part of the country, over millennia, has suffered so much, the names Zebulun and Naphtali became associated with the shame, suffering, darkness, and helplessness of that region.

One could argue that the people who lived there didn't suffer more than anyone else, but Zebulun and Naphtali became a frame of reference for people who were in the greatest need. So it's interesting to note that, centuries before Jesus was born, Isaiah prophesied that the Messiah would burst forth there. The light of God would shine in the darkness—in this place most shamed by the way in which they had failed to withstand the invaders, most shamed by the way in which they had adopted and adapted to pagan ways, in some epochs against their will.

What is the "darkness" of which Isaiah spoke? Darkness is the absence of light, and any dictionary will tell you that it has many applications. Darkness can refer to a lack of understanding or lack of clarity. It can describe a vacuum without moral or spiritual values. Darkness can also refer to a place of uncertainty and confusion. When we're alone in the dark, we wonder about what's out there. We can become paralyzed by fear, ingrown, and obsessed with survival because we fear what's waiting in the dark. Into that kind of a world Jesus came, and He was light.

Light is the opposite of darkness. Light brings clarity and understanding. Light helps people feel secure and know how to move forward, because they are able to see what's beyond themselves. Of course, light can reveal good things and bad things. My garage right now is a winter mess. When the weather is temperate, I leave my garage door open and often sweep it out, keeping it all neat and tidy; but in the winter when temperatures are cold, I don't want the door open. Leaves get tracked in; we keep our pets there when we're away. That's where we store Christmas boxes we haven't thrown away as well as a string of lights I haven't returned to the attic. And wouldn't you know it? My light bulb has burned out in the garage. And I'm not so anxious to replace it. Why? Because when I do, I will not be able to avoid the reality of the mess in there. Sometimes a light can reveal, even in unwelcome ways, the problems and challenges of our lives.

Matthew says that Jesus is God's light; he means that the Lord will reveal the mess of our lives. But He will not just leave us looking at the mess. He will help us clean it up. We see Him working on our behalf and can be inspired to pick up a broom and get to work, too. The light of Jesus calls the best out of us. He shows us the reality of not just who we are, but what we can be. This brings us to the remainder of the text.

## Be a Life-Changer

Jesus is walking along the seashore of Galilee when He sees a group of fishermen at work. He speaks to them in their own language, using a metaphor drawn from their own vocation, to help them understand they can be so much more than what they are. In a real sense, He asks them, "Why are you alive? What's your reason for being?" Who and what do you want to be?

Let me pose the question to you differently. What do you think about most often during the day? When you wake up, what are you thinking about? In the middle of the day, what are you thinking about? At the end of the day, what are you thinking about? When you go to sleep, what are you thinking about? Chances are you have a thread of continuity in those thoughts.

In our midweek men's study, I recently shared the results of a survey that asked, "How often in the day do you think about sex?" What do you suppose the researchers found? They found that, on the average, women think about sex once a day. Men responded quite differently. The researchers found that men thought about sex an average of thirty-three times a day.

Is sex what you think about when you wake up, when you're having lunch, when you're going to sleep? The truth is, some people do.

Others keep thinking about food. They wake up wondering, *What am I going to eat?* At lunch, *What am I going to eat?* At dinner, *What am I going to eat?* Before they go to sleep, *What snack will I reach for before I crawl into bed?*

Maybe your thoughts keep returning to your children because you're a parent. All day long you're thinking about your kids. *How am I going to raise them? What are they doing? Are they safe? How will I invest in them?*

Maybe you keep thinking about your spouse. Maybe it's about your job. Maybe it's about money. We all have these continuing threads of thought. And when someone asks, "Why are you alive?" the answer is probably found in what you're thinking about. That is the reason you're alive. And yet, you can be more than that. You could change the world.

Jesus knew what Simon and Andrew were thinking about—fish. The same story is told in Luke 5, and in that account Jesus has stepped into a boat and is preaching from it. As He reaches the end of His lesson, He says to Simon, "Go out and cast your net into the deep." Simon says, "I've been fishing all night and didn't get anywhere. I've been thinking about fish all night, all day. It's a dead end. I'm thinking right now about what a failure I am as a fisherman."

But Jesus says, "Go out and cast your net over there in the deep." Simon does, and his crew pulls up the net filled with so many fish that it begins to break. Then Jesus looks at them and says, "Follow me, and I'll make you fishers of people." Simon and his brother Andrew get out of the boat and walk away with Him.

Whatever you're thinking about, you can think about more. Whatever you're doing, you can do more. We all can be fixated on our little corner of the world, but Jesus calls us to reach the world itself.

Everyone knows the name Steve Jobs, the genius who birthed and raised Apple, the most valuable company in the world today (as measured in dollars and cents). In the early 1980s, he developed the Macintosh computer, a formidable achievement in itself. Still, he had bigger dreams. He went to John Sculley, the president of PepsiCo, and asked him to come on board as the CEO of Apple. Sculley said, "I don't want to do it. I'm happy at Pepsi Cola." Pepsi was challenging Coca-Cola as the preeminent beverage of our time and making real strides toward that end.

Steve Jobs wanted Sculley's marketing expertise and acumen to propel computers into the future. (Remember, in the 1980s few people imagined they'd ever have a computer in their home.) So Jobs looked him straight in the eye and asked, "Are you telling me you would rather give your life to making sugared water instead of changing the world?"

You know what happened? Sculley quit Pepsi, became the CEO at Apple, and remained so for the next ten years, as Apple cemented its place as a leader in high-tech business. The point is this: most of us are content with making sugared water when we could be changing the world. Don't tell me that you can't do it. Don't tell me that you're not worthy, you're not able, or you're not gifted. Don't tell me that you're a failure, your parents didn't like you, your schoolteacher scorned you, your friends made fun of you, your spouse left you, or your children think you're a jerk. When God comes into your life, you can Jesus B. You can do more than influence others, you can show what it means to live in right relationship with God and help them see the world as heaven sees it.

This is your calling. If you commit yourself to following Jesus, you are committed to influencing other people. It's not enough for you to walk through the world, not caring what happens to others. It's not enough for you to receive the truth, not caring if others understand it. It's not enough for you to go from your cradle to your grave being true to your own values and principles. You must change the course of other people's lives. That is what Jesus calls you to do, so you can do it.

"Oh, but I'm not a preacher," you say. You don't have to be. "I'm not a teacher." You don't have to be. "I'm not the head of the corporate ladder." You don't have to be. You just have to Jesus B. "Follow me, and I will cause you to change people's lives." You see, if you become a Jesus follower, you will wake up in the morning thinking, *Who am I going to bless and change today?* When you go to lunch, you will wonder, *Who am I going to bless and change this afternoon?* When you go to sleep, you will be thinking, *When I wake up tomorrow, how is God going to use me to change someone else for the good?*

Many people who profess to follow Christ do not think this way, and consequently miss the power and promise that the disciples of Galilee discovered. They believe they are following Jesus, but they go through their days not blessing people or calling the best out of them. Instead they push others down, perhaps even feed their neuroses or cause them to look more darkly on their world instead of seeing it with more light. We all know people who seem to have a predisposition to see the glass half empty. For them, "It's never going to work; I'm never going to have a chance; people have always done me wrong; I'm always going to be left out; I'll never have life as good as someone else." Sadly, some would-be Christ-followers feed these cynical and self-defeating ideas in their own hearts and the hearts of others.

## See What God Can Do through You

For many years as a Senior Pastor, I was part of a group of pastors from across the country who met together during the first week of February every year, visiting a church ministry larger and more sweeping than any of ours. It was a rich and life-giving fellowship for me that I still miss, as my ministry assignment has changed.

One year, we stopped by several large churches in Atlanta, one of which was in the suburb named Buckhead. This congregation had moved into a new $36 million building, with an auditorium seating three thousand. I asked a member of its staff, "How do you fill up those seats? Do you have a schedule of multiple services?"

"Oh, no," he replied. "It's half empty. We're so excited!"

I thought, *What? You spent $36 million, incurred no small debt, endured the stress that clothes every building project of any magnitude, and all the rest, to build a place that's half empty? And you're excited? I don't get it.*

He must have seen my confused grimace. He continued, "In our old place, we were crowded and just couldn't seem to grow anymore. But now we have all these empty seats! Any time we see an empty seat, we see an opportunity to lead someone else to Jesus Christ. As long as we're in ministry, we want to make sure we have empty seats. If we fill this up, we'll add another service. We'll keep adding services until we fill all the empty seats and, if necessary, we'll get another place."

Well, I came home and noticed a lot of empty seats in our church sanctuary. A visitor could say, "This church isn't going anywhere. What's up with these people? I'm not going to attend a church that's half empty." Or the same person could say, "Hundreds of people are going to get saved here, and God has put their chairs in place even before we know who they are."

You can look at everything in life differently. You can look at your hometown and say it's not going anywhere. You can see your job as a dead end. You can see your neighbors as dull, uninteresting people. Or you can wake up in the morning and say, "Today, I'm going to Jesus B. I'm going to call the best out of somebody. I'm going to help them see the world beyond themselves. I'm going to help them see what they can do with God, how they can bless somebody else. I'm not going to feed their whining and complaining. I'm going to listen and help them appreciate their circumstances. I am, like Jesus, going to be life-giving light."

Jesus says, "Follow me, and I'll cause you to become fishers of people. You'll be casting out your net every day and pulling in people. Your life can be so much more than you ever imagined."

You can choose not to Jesus B. You can choose to just survive, just plan your next meal, or build your financial fortune. You can go to bed tonight and wake up tomorrow morning thinking about your stock portfolio. You can focus your thoughts and activities on making money and growing your business. Or you can choose to think, *How can I use my business to bless other people? How can I share my next meal with someone who needs Jesus?*

See how it works? Wherever God has placed you, in whatever scenario you find yourself, if you want to Jesus B., you will influence other people to follow Him, too. In so doing, you're going to be light in their darkness. You're going to be the person from whom others walk away saying, "I feel so much better because of that conversation; man, that guy (or gal) always takes me somewhere new, hopeful, better."

Yes, the light sometimes reveals a messy garage. Sometimes we have to acknowledge, "That life is a mess." But never, ever leave it there. Speak into that life positively, not with condemnation, but hope. Let others know you hear them and that you know life is not easy and has become a mess for them. But, be sure to reassure them that, with God, even the Devil's mischief can be turned for the good. Never leave a conversation with another person in despair; always leave them with hope.

*But that's not realistic*, you may be thinking. *It's wrong to give people false hope.* I say that as long as God is on the throne, hope is real, tangible, and powerful. If the worst that's said about you when you go to your grave is, "That person was always talking about how things could work out. That person was always hopeful," you will have done well. Jesus B. will have become your signature.

You make the call. Who will you be? Jesus says, "Follow me and you'll call the best out of other people. You'll become their light on a dark, cloudy day." Jesus Christ calls you and me, not merely to imitate Him, but to model for others His life and light.

# 4. JESUS B. THE HEALER

One thing I enjoyed about living in Seattle was the proximity of the city to the wilderness. You can drive 35 or 40 miles from the very heart of the urban core and find yourself in deep wilderness, where trees are tall and the glacial-fed whitewater streams run rapidly down to the Puget Sound. While our boys were young, Maureen and I decided to take them on a picnic with another couple from our church who had two children in the same age range as our four sons. We traveled into the lower elevations of the Cascade Mountains, following Interstate 90 eastbound from its beginning in downtown Seattle at the edge of Elliott Bay for about 40 miles.

As we got off the interstate on a forest service road, we found ourselves clothed with the fresh scent of evergreen under a crisp, clean, blue sky, nearing the Wenatchee National Forest. Denny Creek is a picture-perfect small river, less than a hundred feet wide and not very deep. Whitewater rushes westward from the melting snowline of spring and summer, high above; the water is cold as ice because, well, it was ice not so long before. There are tall trees everywhere, reaching for the heavens. The groundcover of Pacific Northwest forests is not dense, making walking beneath the trees relatively easy, but the trees grow together in such a way as to inhibit direct sunlight and rainfall on the ground below. Hansel and Gretel could find the gingerbread house in the neighborhood of Denny Creek. Parking our cars at the end of the dirt and gravel road, deep in the woods, we walked along a path toward the sound of the flowing river, its splashing roar against the boulders and rocks that define the riverbed growing louder with each step.

Because it was a hot day, Denny Creek seemed the ideal spot for a picnic. As we found our way to the creek's shore, the kids wanted to cross straightway and Jacob, who was our oldest son (at that time in the fourth grade), led the way. My wife, Maureen, and the other young mom on the outing with us, waited in the grassy meadow and sun-drenched clearing that had become our picnic ground, with baby Nathanael, while Andrew, our third son, and I brought up the rear of the line of hikers. Andrew was then four years old. As we approached the creek I held his hand, so that he could keep up and cross safely. But Andrew became afraid as he sized up the swift-moving water and surveyed the rocks and obstacles around which it moved. He cried out, "Daddy, Daddy!" So I picked him up, set him on my shoulders, and we began to walk across the creek as one.

As we reached the middle of the creek, drinking in the spectacular beauty of the whole stage, bathed by warm sunshine, and laughing and talking with my friend who was crossing with his two children, the world seemed perfect, and, if but for a moment, without flaw. Focused on everything but where I stepped with my feet, I slipped on a rock and began to fall. I feared I would fall on Andrew, so I twisted and fell the other way to protect him. I landed in the creek bed on my shoulder, suddenly immersed in the most excruciating pain I have ever known. I have been spared serious accident or illness for a lifetime, but in that minute I tasted devastating, inescapable, mind-bending physical pain.

I was not sure of its cause or even what had exactly happened; all I knew was that my whole body was electrified with intense pain, even as I understood I needed to keep Andrew's head above the water. Stunned, I was not sure what to do next. I clambered up out of the water as best I could, reeling. Maureen ran out and grabbed Andrew so I could limp back to the shore. By the time I got back to the riverbank, I was semi-conscious and beginning to black out.

I have very little memory of what happened next. I remember riding in the car, leaning against the passenger side door and moaning as Maureen careened down the mountain highway to nearby village called North Bend, in which a hospital could be found. I remember that my shoulder and arm hurt, desperately, and I was somehow unable to hold them together. I remember being laid out on a gurney in the emergency room.

I was wearing a pullover polo shirt (one of my favorites); I remember a doctor saying, "Hey, guy, I think we're going to have to cut your shirt off."

"Don't cut my shirt," I protested, with a mumble. "It's my favorite shirt." But scissors in hand, he sliced the polo from neck to navel anyway. After that, I blacked out again—or maybe I was silenced with anesthesia.

When I woke up, sprawled on a table facing the ceiling, the doctor stood over me and explained, "Your shoulder was dislocated, but we've reset it back into place."

"I had surgery?"

"No. We just manipulated it back into place. It will be all right. It will be sore for a while, but it will be fine. Just watch it. Once it pops out, it may pop out again." Maureen drove me home, both of us amazed that I had escaped a night in the hospital, given what might have been a more serious injury.

Reflecting on that day's events, I also have one more vivid memory. I know I screamed, in the deepest pain, "Dear Jesus, heal me!"

When our bodies hurt, everything else fades into the distance—all of us know that's true—and we are fixed on finding relief. For me, that day, the emergency room doctor was the very person of Jesus, because he relieved my suffering. He took away the pain that was paralyzing. I didn't understand what was wrong with my body. I only knew that I had fallen and could not continue as I was; the pain was more than I could manage at the time. The doctor took my pain away, as the Gospels tell us that Jesus did for many whose paths He crossed as He walked in this world.

One reason Jesus towers over history is because He was the consummate healer. We all know that He was a miracle worker. He was a great teacher, and I love to read about His teaching. Supernatural phenomena attended His life: angels sang on the night of His birth and at different points in His life journey, God spoke from the heavens authenticating His words and office as others heard it like the sound of thunder, and so on. But the stories of Jesus most deeply impressed in my memory are those of His healing ministry. Those are the ones with which I connect when my life is spinning out of control and I'm paralyzed by the pain all around me.

The question we often ask is, "How can I be healed?" We seldom ask, "How can I be the healer?" I suppose this reflects the preoccupation and self-centeredness of our faith. We tend to run to Jesus when we want something from Him—and, fairly, He invites us to do so. There's no shame in so doing. But if that's all we do, are we faithfully following Christ? Are we fully living up to His call upon our lives? It's not enough to ask, "How can I be healed?"—though that question may be appropriate at times—we should also ask, "How can I be the healer? When I see others suffering, how can I Jesus B.?"

Let us take a look at a couple of Jesus' healing stories from Matthew 8:

*When Jesus returned to Capernaum, a Roman officer came and pleaded with him, "Lord, my young servant lies in bed paralyzed and in terrible pain." Jesus said, "I will come and heal him." But the officer said, "Lord, I am not worthy to have you come into my home. Just say the word from where you are and my servant will be healed. I know this because I am under the authority of my superior officers, and I have authority over my soldiers. I only need to say, 'Go,' and they go or, 'Come,' and they come. And if I say to my slaves, 'Do this,' they do it." When Jesus heard this he was amazed. Turning to those who were following him, he said, "I tell you the truth. I haven't seen faith like this in all Israel! And I tell you this, that many Gentiles will come from all over the world—from east and west—and sit down with Abraham, Isaac, and Jacob at the feast of the Kingdom of Heaven. But many Israelites—those for whom the Kingdom was prepared—will be thrown into outer darkness, where there will be weeping and gnashing of teeth." Then Jesus said to the Roman officer, "Go back home. Because you have believed, it has happened." And the young servant was healed that same hour. (vv 5-13)*

*When Jesus arrived at Peter's house, Peter's mother-in-law was sick in bed with a high fever. But when Jesus touched her hand, the fever left her. Then she got up and prepared a meal for him. That evening, many demon-possessed people were brought to Jesus. He cast out the evil spirits with a simple command, and he healed all the sick. This fulfilled the word of the Lord through the prophet Isaiah, who said, "He took our sicknesses and removed our diseases." (vv 14-17)*

Jesus was a wonder-worker. He intervened in people's lives supernaturally. He caused things to happen that no known medicine could bring to pass. He could speak in a place and someone who was not even physically present could be healed. He could stand removed from the situation and still effect a physical restoration that no human reason can explain. He was able to come to a sick person, like Peter's mother-in-law, and to touch and heal that person. By different methodologies (the speaking of a word, by the touching of a hand, in the communication of His Spirit), He was able to effect supernatural healing.

Some argue that the healing ministry of Jesus is no longer operative in this world, that its efficacy was a unique season in human history. They say that divine healing characterized a unique era when Jesus Himself, in the flesh, walked in this world, and, for various reasons, God chose to work through Him in this material world in a supernatural way. But now that He has ascended to the right hand of the Father, those promises of healing are no longer operative.

Another understanding of these stories says, no, Jesus intended to model for us what we might also do. I lean toward this understanding of the text, because Jesus specifically says to His disciples in another place, "If you've been amazed at what you've seen Me do, well, get ready, because you're going to do the same things I've done" (John 14:12, para.). I believe that the power of the Holy Spirit can fall upon a believer's life and empower that person to be like Jesus—not simply to have Christlike virtues (such as a readiness to forgive), but to be able to supernaturally alter the course of events and circumstances in the world here and now.

We are the body of Christ. We are His hands until He comes back. We are His voice until He comes back. We are filled with the Holy Spirit of Jesus that can actually give us the mind of Christ, the understanding of Christ, and the perspective of Christ. The Scripture tells us that the Holy Spirit equips us supernaturally for the work of God in the kingdom. And the Scripture specifically tells us, in books like 1 Corinthians, that one of those gifts is a gift of healing (1 Cor 12:28-30).

Allow me to state it plainly: I believe it is possible for God to supernaturally heal us today. Furthermore, it is possible for members of the body of Christ to be equipped by the Holy Spirit with a supernatural gift to heal. That is not to say that all of us will have such a gift (1 Cor 12:30), but there is a present reality of supernatural physical healing. The power of the Holy Spirit can equip individuals by the Spirit's appointment with that healing power. Furthermore, I contend that the gift of healing, like other spiritual gifts, may be for a lifetime or may be for a season.

Sometimes people imagine that a supernatural gift signifies a fixed assignment for life, like an appointment to the Supreme Court. They forget that the gifts exist to further the kingdom enterprise. In God's supernatural wisdom, He may equip you with a gift for a season and that gift may then be removed or go dormant. It's God's gift to you for God's purposes. It is not your plaything.

All of that to say, you may be called and equipped to serve as an agent of supernatural healing in a season, but may not have it as a lifetime call. You may be someone who has a lifetime gift of healing, but you may not be. You may never be an instrument of God's supernatural healing in the way that Jesus healed the centurion's servant or Peter's mother-in-law. But even without that gift you can still Jesus B.

Have you ever thought of yourself as Jesus the healer? I think the texts from Matthew 8, when seen through the lens of God's supernatural gifting, reveal other angles with which to draw truth from these stories. I've heard many sermons about the faith of the centurion, Jesus' amazement at his faith (in spite of the fact that he was a Gentile), and so on. All of these insights are appropriate because the text plainly states these truths. However, on this passage, I do not believe I have ever heard an exposition that explored how we might continue Jesus' ministry of healing. How can we be like that? How could we do that? How could we be God's instruments of healing?

Our world needs healing today, so I encourage you to be a healer as Jesus was. But how can you? How?

## Wait for an Invitation

The first thing that strikes me about the centurion's story is that Jesus heals by invitation. The centurion approaches him and seeks his help. By contrast, we are often busybodies;

we try to intervene in other people's lives when we've had no invitation to do so. Sometimes we think that it's our right to diagnose other people's problems and prescribe their cures. We believe we are called to straighten up other people's lives, to advise them how to sort out their tortured spiritual journey.

Jesus had a word for people like this: *hypocrites*. His counsel? "First get rid of the log in your own eye; then you will see well enough to deal with the speck in your friend's eye" (Matt 7:5). My life is so complex that I don't need to think about how I am going to sort out your world if you do not seek my help. On the other hand, I do want to come alongside you if you ask. If I want to Jesus B., especially Jesus the healer, then I should respond to the invitations that I receive from hurting people. There are indeed people inviting us to help them if we'll just pay attention—people all around us, all the time—but let's not waste time trying to solve the problems of people who haven't asked us for help and don't really desire it in the first place.

Truth be told, some people will ask for help but then refuse to take it. How many people go to doctors and pay a large diagnostic fee, then walk out of the office and say, "Well, I'm not doing that! I really want to be well, but I'm not taking that medicine. I'm not going to follow that regime." Some of my own parishioners have told me stories like that. It's a part of the human condition. We have desperate hours during which we desperately want help, but we are reluctant to surrender control of our lives, even if such a surrender is necessary to receive the help we crave and the wholeness and healing it can bring.

You cannot be a healer unless someone wants you to be. Even if you are a physician who receives a handsome fee, your efforts will not make any difference for patients whose hearts are not open to the remedy you offer.

As a pastor, I have often counseled and prayed with people who had all kinds of fears and doubts and traumas. I'd say, "Well, based on what you've told me and as I understand it, this is what Scripture says you should do." Then some have said, "Well, I'm not doing that. Thanks, but no thanks."

Our capacity to heal someone in Jesus' name always depends on the heart of the person who needs to be healed. Maybe that's why Jesus could not heal many people in His hometown—because they didn't have faith in Him. They didn't expect Him to be their healer. Perhaps, that is why Jesus still does not solve many problems that He is altogether equipped to solve—because some sufferers will not invite Him to intervene and, even when they do, they will not follow His instructions. This is why Jesus often asked prospective patients if they truly wanted to be healed (Mark 10:51; John 5:6).

## Be Involved; Be Authentic

The centurion trusted Jesus, though we have no indication that he had any previous contact with Christ. How could he have known about Jesus and had such confidence in Him? Because Jesus had demonstrated over time the integrity of His soul and witness. He was anchored already in the centurion's world even though the centurion only knew about Him from a distance. If you want to be a healer like Jesus, you must be committed to a consistent, authentic, anchoring presence in the world you hope to serve. Over time, trust is developed. People begin to see and understand that you are genuinely interested in restoring them to wholeness. Though you are flawed in ways Jesus never was, it's still possible that, over time, people will look past your flaws to the nature of your heart. They will begin to trust you if you are that kind of anchoring presence.

Your good intentions will be rejected at times. You cannot simply shrink back into a cave when wounded. You should not try to escape from all the painful experiences of serving in Jesus' name. You should not just go where your work will be affirmed. You cannot just move around all the time, never sure of where you are. You cannot heal a world in which you are known, but unpredictable. Jesus was steady. He was faithful. He was true. He was consistent. No wonder the centurion seeks Jesus in a desperate hour; this is the one person he can trust to take his need seriously. If you want to be a healer, you must be a person upon whom others can depend.

## Spread Hope

I think the centurion also reached out to Jesus because He was a hope-giving personality. He called light out of people's darkness. If you would Jesus B., you must also be that radiant hope of life. No matter what the circumstance, no matter how dark the hour, how impossible the scenario, how tall the mountain, how broad the river, or how deep the pain, you have a word of hope to share: *There is a God.* God can intervene. God can make things right. God can heal. God loves us, cares for us, and is gracious to us—no matter how desperate or impossible our plight.

This was the emphasis of Jesus' conversation and teaching. Jesus did not spend a lot of time identifying other people's faults or groaning about how people did not pay attention to Him. So far as we know, He never wrestled with the fact that His work could have spread more rapidly if He had only been born in Rome. He did not drag other people down, making them discouraged when He faced discouraging circumstances. Jesus was in every minute a voice of hope. If you want to be a healer, you must a voice of hope, as well.

Sad to say, too many people who fill our church chairs and auditoriums are not voices of hope. They want to know how they can be healed, but they heal no one. All they can speak about are their woes, their occasions of sadness, the faults of others, the disappointments of life, the failed and unmet expectations, all the difficulties and challenges they face. Even when they smile, it's a kind of smile framed by sadness or frustration or both. I think Jesus brought life into every room He entered.

He inspired hope. Do you want to be a healer like Jesus? Be steady, be consistent, be life-affirming, and be hope-giving.

## Listen to Others' Needs

Another way in which Jesus was a healer was that He listened. He truly listened. Of course, we do not have the whole conversation recorded, but I'm going to guess there was more to what the centurion told Jesus about his ailing servant than Matthew penned. "I value this man so much," I can hear the centurion say. "He helped me one day when my chariot broke down, and I was waylaid by the roadside. I can depend on him to care for my family when I have to travel for days and weeks at a time, as my employer calls me away." He may have said much more, and I'm sure that his comments impressed upon Jesus the sacredness of this man's relationship to his servant. The centurion saw him as more than a servant; he saw him as a friend or even a family member. Jesus heard that. He heard the man's anguish and heart cry.

My physician is Scott Green. When I first moved to Anderson, several members of the church's search committee (that brought me to town) recommended him to me when I inquired about healthcare. I did not know Scott at all, but he has become my friend because he excels at listening to me, his patient. He probably knows me better—and knows more about me—than he would like to know. Conversely, he likely knows more about me than I want him to know. I have stood before him, figuratively and literally, naked, without so much as a fig leaf. But, I trust him. I believe that Scott will never use what he knows about me to harm me, but, instead, only to help and to heal me. And his capacity to help me is hinged on his willingness to listen to me. In any normal course of treatment, a physician will never be able to provide you with the medicine you need unless he or she *hears* you. Similarly, you will not be able to heal anyone until you listen. *Carefully.*

Jesus was the consummate listener. As He listened, He expressed His willingness to get involved. He volunteered to help. He reassured the centurion that He was so interested in his servant's need that He would interrupt His journey. He would change His schedule. He would postpone the good He intended to do at His destination in order to help this man. So it is for you and me. If we want to Jesus B., we must communicate to people that we care for them so much that we're willing to interrupt our ordinary course to help them. If we want to Jesus B., we must be willing to respond immediately to the cry for help—willing to go to the place of need, even if we must interrupt what we had planned.

## Speak Healing

Here's the part of the narrative truth for us that I think is most important: Jesus heals as He speaks. He speaks words of healing. He tells the centurion, "Don't worry. After listening to your story and observing the quality of your heart and understanding the circumstances, I am speaking a word of healing right now. *Your servant is well.* God is on the throne, and He is doing this great thing, so I am confident to speak this word of healing. It will take place." And so it does.

When He arrives at His destination, Jesus touches Peter's mother-in-law with a compassionate, healing touch (Matt 8:14-15). Jesus is always projecting healing. He speaks it. He demonstrates it. He expresses it even in His touch. Even if we are not equipped by the Holy Spirit with a supernatural gift to effect physical healing, in this broken world all of us in the body of Christ can Jesus B. the healer by speaking words of healing. We can speak in a way that affirms the power of God to mend and make whole, we can speak words that inspire faith, and if necessary we can challenge sufferers to accept the healing of God.

In popular parlance, we might call this constructive conversation or problem-solving conversation. If there is any scourge in this community, any scourge in the body of Christ, any scourge in ordinary human relationships, it's our tendency to identify and articulate what's broken in someone's life without identifying or offering a constructive solution. Problem-solving is healing, and healing breathes hope and wholeness.

There is a God. I may not be sure how the answer to a person's affliction will appear, but I know this: God is the answer. I may not anticipate how God's answer will unfold, but I know this: If my words and actions are dedicated to God, they will unfold for His glory, and when God is glorified, His people are blessed. When someone asks me to pray for their healing, I may not know how things will work out, but I do know that I can speak words of healing into their circumstance.

When feelings are wounded, I can disturb someone's wound so that it bleeds again or I can be a healing balm. I can allow someone's wound to fester and let the infection worsen, or I can be a healing ointment. I can heighten someone's distress and feed their misery by enabling their dysfunction, or I can speak words of recovery. "Come and drink" (Isa 55:1). "Seek the Lord while you can find Him. Call on him now while He is near" (Isa 55:6). "Then you will have healing for your body and strength for your bones" (Prov 3:8). Jesus was the consummate healer because He was supremely confident in the power of God over all of His creation, even the power to heal. We can have that confidence as well.

You see, you can say very encouraging things, but if you do not believe what you are saying, your words will not have much effect in others' lives. You must say what you believe. To speak without authenticity is just beating the air, but if you believe:

- There is a God who is still working in this world,
- That God can supernaturally do for the good what no human being thinks possible, and
- That God can speak a miraculous answer into the most desperate hour,

...then you can speak words of healing. Jesus did. Whether it was the centurion's servant, Peter's mother-in-law, blind Bartimaeus by the roadside, the paralyzed man by the Pool of Bethesda, or Lazarus in the tomb, Jesus responded to invitations to heal. He listened. He expressed His willingness to help. He spoke words of healing, and He believed what He said. He even communicated healing with His touch.

Do you want to Jesus B. the healer? Do you want to move past your own aches and pains to become a divine agent of relief from pain? I do. As I walk through my world, I want things to be mended in my wake, not broken. I want scars to be made whole, not reopened. I want to Jesus B. a giver of hope and healing. I think you can, too, if you're willing.

# 5. JESUS B. FRIEND OF SINNERS

I understand that I'll never be the Savior of the world, and neither will you. None of us are perfect enough to take anyone else's fault on ourselves in a way to satisfy the claim of the universe. Whenever we do something wrong, whenever we disobey God, whenever our more base nature leads us into conduct or thoughts unworthy of our Creator, justice demands that a price be paid. No one can pay that price for someone else, unless the substitute is morally perfect.

This is the story of Jesus, of course. Jesus is perfect, so He was able to take all of our sin upon Himself. He willingly laid down His own life and suffered so that we might escape that same suffering, so that we might escape the sentence of death, eternally. He took it on Himself. Only Jesus could do that, and we will never be Jesus in that way. But we can be Jesus in some very important ways until He returns at the last day. One way is to "seek and save the lost." We can befriend wayward people and point them to Christ, who can restore them to full relationship with God.

Matthew 9 tells us how Jesus did this with a man named Matthew. We do not know whether the original disciple named Matthew wrote this book that bears his name, although the church's tradition has always contended that he is, in fact, the one who penned its lines. Regardless of its authorship, this Gospel is a compelling collection of stories about what Jesus said and did during His earthly ministry. What better place to learn about Jesus' first contact with Matthew? The Bible text says:

> As Jesus was walking along, he saw a man named Matthew sitting at his tax collector's booth. "Follow me and be my disciple," Jesus said to him. So Matthew got up and followed him. Later, Matthew invited Jesus and his disciples to his home as dinner guests, along with many tax collectors and other disreputable sinners. But when the Pharisees saw this, they asked his disciples, "Why does your Teacher eat with such scum?" When Jesus heard this, he said, "Healthy people don't need a doctor—sick people do." Then he added, "Now go and learn the meaning of this Scripture: 'I want you to show mercy, not offer sacrifices.' For I have come to call not those who think they are righteous, but those who know they are sinners." (vv 9–13)

## Ministry by Walking Around

If you and I want to be like Jesus, we need to be out, in the everyday world, walking around. Jesus never closeted Himself with a community of people who already agreed with Him. He was never cloistered or isolated from an unbelieving world so He could simply enjoy the company of people who were already persuaded that He was the Messiah. He never separated Himself from the hustle and bustle and tumult of life. He did not avoid the soiled, grimy, desperate, and hopeless people along life's road. He was not sequestered from things that were not happy and pretty. He was out in the world, walking with, watching for, listening to, and seeking to find lost people.

Jesus was on the road to Jericho. We find Him in the culturally hostile territory of Samaria, and we find Him in the bustle of His own capital city, Jerusalem. He can be found in His modest hometown of Nazareth. He spent time in the busy fishing village of Capernaum, where He established a home. He walked along the seashore of Galilee—and as far away as Syro-Phoenicia, in Tyre, now within the modern boundary of Lebanon.

Jesus traveled everywhere on foot. He did not have a car, a motorcycle, or even a horse. But He goes as far as anybody could go with a pair of feet. Although His disciples try to guard Him from the curious crowds, He often turns aside from the agreed itinerary to talk with someone of interest. When parents surround Him with their children, His disciples try to intervene, but He says, "Back off. Let the little ones come to Me."

When those not spiritually framed in the accepted sense, despised by and despising religious do-gooders, Gentiles and "notorious sinners," came to see Him, He was not troubled. Jesus seemed to have complete liberty to associate with all kinds of people in this world. If I want to be Jesus, I need to exercise that same freedom.

Matthew's Gospel often describes Jesus as "walking," and I think that verb is significant. He literally had His feet on the ground where common people live. He did not live above them. He did not live apart from them. He lived with them. He rubbed shoulders with them, watched them, and engaged them in conversation about their daily activities.

As Jesus was out and about, He was not lost in His own thoughts. I am an introvert, so even in the midst of a large crowd, I may be completely oblivious to my surroundings. Sometimes at the YMCA, where I run five days a week, I intersect with other people without being truly aware of them. A week later, someone may say, "Remember what I told you at the Y?" But I do not remember the conversation, because I was so focused on myself and my own exercise routine. I run like an obsessive guinea pig on a little track above the gym, so I scarcely know anyone else is there. "Were you playing basketball?" I ask. "Were you on the track?" Sometimes people will say, "Sorry, I didn't mean to get in your way. You almost ran me over." I admit that I can be very self-absorbed. I can be lost in my own world, swirling about in my own head alone. I might have the freedom to go here and there as Jesus did, but I'm not likely to connect with people just by walking around without intentionally seeking to do so.

## Jesus' Ideal Relationship

What was Jesus watching for as He walked around? Most of us watch for the newest car, the latest fashion, or something entertaining on the horizon. Jesus did not look for trends or fads. He seemed completely nonplused by the things that routinely make our heads turn. Jesus watched broken hearts. Read all four of the Gospels and you will see this pattern: day-by-day, His attention was arrested by people who had broken hearts.

Jesus' object in watching other people is different from yours or mine. For instance, Jesus is not looking for people who can bring Him some personal benefit. Think about that. He never seems to think, *If I get close to this person, he might be able to help me accomplish what I want. I might look better if I'm next to her. I might go farther if they are my friends. I might have some advantage if they come to work in my company. If I am in their circle, their good reputation will reflect on me.*

We're loath to admit it, but many of us calculate the value of our relationships in those ways. We want to be with people we think will advance our cause, our sense of self-worth, or our sense of personal value. We want to be in the company of people who can do something for us, open a door of opportunity for us. Jesus never seems to be concerned about such things. Maybe that's because He doesn't need anything. He's so complete that He doesn't need to draw help from anyone.

Yet we understand from the Scripture that God's nature longs for relationship. God seeks communion with those He has created in His image who willingly choose Him as a friend and companion, a soul mate, so to speak. We see this in the

Creation account, the life stories of the patriarchs, and else-where. It may be fair to say that while God needs nothing from us, God does long for a relationship with us.

So it is with Jesus, Who is the exact representation of God. He does not need anything from anyone, but He still desires an intimate relationship with us. Jesus' pursuit of relationships is not based on what He will receive but on what He can give. In other words, He seeks a holy relationship. Jesus is not looking to receive anything from others, but He strives to establish relationships that are healthy and life-giving.

## "What Will Others Say?"

There's another sense in which Jesus was not like us, as He pursued and developed relationships. He seemed completely unconcerned about what other people would say about the company He kept. He was not concerned about what the re-ligious establishment would say or what the politicians would say or what respectable business people would say or even what His disciples or family members would say. He was not cautious or calculating when thinking of how others might talk or draw conclusions based on those He chose to befriend. He was able to live above and without regard for the constant drone of public opinion.

You might say you're not concerned about what others think either, but that's unlikely. In fact, all of us have some sense of how we're perceived, and we're conscious of it; more often than we would like to admit, we worry about it. Many of us want to please others at a very fundamental part of our being, so it's hard for us to see potential relationships as clearly as Jesus did. We are not simply concerned about what we can do for someone else; we are also concerned about how other people will interpret our involvement.

As a pastor, I wrestled with that dynamic for thirty years. A lot of people were watching me and noticing the people with whom I associated. I received some pretty sharp criticism from well-meaning people who felt it was not appropriate for me to be in the company of certain people. "Oh, we agree, Pastor, that you should be civil to everyone," they'd say, "but don't become friends with this person because, well, that might be bad for the church." In fact, I once officiated at a baby dedication for a couple, one of whom had a rather randy reputation in town. I wasn't aware of that until after the baby dedication, when I was challenged by someone who was a fixture in the next-to-the-last row every Sunday, "You'd do anything for a scalp, wouldn't you?"

"What?"

"Well, we all know what kind of person he is. You shouldn't bring that sort forward for a baby dedication. Regardless of what he's says now, today, what are you thinking? Given his reputation, what will others say about us? About the church? About you? Aren't you endorsing him, as if he were living righteously, by parading him up front? What people think matters; we have to protect our witness, our reputation."

I confess I was quite taken aback; my first impulse was to say, "My goodness! I don't want to cause any trouble." But immediately, the Holy Spirit impressed me, powerfully, "What *are you thinking*, Jim Lyon? You are here to welcome anybody who seeks Jesus." And that man, dedicating his baby, was seeking Jesus.

My point is this: all of us have a tendency to worry about what others are going to say or think about us when we reach out to people who are not already followers of Jesus, or whose journey with Jesus has been troubled, but Jesus Himself seemed to be free from such worry. He was not afraid to seek people who were broken. He did not look for people who thought they already had it together; He did not seek people who felt they were righteous already; He did not try to recruit disciples from the ranks of the religious establishment. He looked for those who had been set to the side (or at least felt like they had been set to the side), people who were considered incapable of godly conversation, people rejected by the rest of society as having no or less-than value.

Jesus saw Matthew, a tax collector. In those days, Jews despised tax collectors because they were employees of the Roman government, a foreign occupying power. Their office gave them the ability to abuse their neighbors. They had to collect a base tax for Rome, but on top of that they could add a surcharge for their personal benefit. They could make themselves wealthy at other people's expense, and often did so in a cavalier way. "If you treat me well, I might reduce your tax burden. But if you don't treat me well, I will increase it," their attitude implied. "If you will take my daughter out, you might get a break. But if you tell me she's ugly, you're history." The power of taxation could be used to manipulate all kinds of people in a social environment, and it was. Because of collaboration with the Romans, because of abuse of power, because of the economic inequities rife in such a dysfunctional governing and taxing system, tax collectors had become a class despised. They were considered to be the lowest of the low, the last rung of the ladder or worse. As Jesus walked along the shoreline of the Sea of Galilee, His eyes fell on such a man, Matthew.

Don't pass over this fact lightly: *Jesus sees Matthew.* There must have been a thousand people He could have seen along the road that day, but Jesus fixed His gaze on Matthew. What was it about Matthew? Perhaps they had conversed before. Perhaps there was a preexisting relationship; many people believe that. Perhaps Jesus had heard about Matthew from others along the road, or from His own disciples. Perhaps they had no prior connection, yet on that day Jesus noticed Matthew because He was watching for such people.

And what sort of man did Jesus see? Did He see a kind of quisling, a person who had compromised his loyalty to his own people by being employed by the Romans? Did Jesus assume that Matthew was greedy, because no one would be a tax collector unless driven at some level by greed? Did He see a man soiled and cast off, for good reason? Is that what He saw? No, because Jesus does not see as other people do. I want to see as Jesus does. I want to Jesus B., a friend of sinners and outcasts.

## What Matthew Saw in Jesus

What do you suppose Matthew thought when Jesus approached him? By this time, Jesus was widely known as a wonder-worker. He was a kind of celebrity, so it's unlikely that He walked down the road without being noticed. There was probably a crowd surging around Him, making a commotion. Did Matthew know Jesus personally? Maybe not. But did he know of Jesus? Likely. I imagine that when he saw Jesus, Matthew quickly turned away because he didn't really want to engage Him in any sort of conversation. This fellow was different, and Matthew may not have felt worthy of talking with Him. (He would never admit that out loud, of course, but deep down inside he probably was ashamed of what he'd made of his life. So I believe Matthew looked away when Jesus looked right at him.)

When Jesus came over, Matthew may have busied himself arranging the gold coins on his desk or the elegant fabrics of his customs house. Maybe he was just tidying up. I say this because, when we don't want to face the truth about ourselves, we'll find ways to be busy. As Jesus came up, Matthew may have made quick conversation, hoping to take the advantage. "Oh, you must be Jesus, the wonder-worker. I've heard about you. Yeah, big deal. Have you paid your taxes?" All kinds of bluster. Maybe he was overbearing. Maybe he began to wander off and talk about how he used to go to synagogue back in the old days, but it was such a dud that he just didn't go anymore. "It was so boring! Who needs that?"

We don't know exactly how Matthew acted when Jesus approached him, but Jesus saw something there. Obviously Jesus saw something that nobody else did, because Jesus, in that conversation, summarized for us in one brief phrase what He knew Matthew should do. He said, "Matthew, follow Me." So much was implied in that phrase: "Why don't you take My side? Why don't you come over to where I am? Why don't you walk with Me and become a part of My circle? Come on, Matthew. You do not have to sit here for the rest of your life. You do not have to live this way. You do not have to be ostracized. You do not have to feel guilty for associating with our oppressors. You do not have to keep going on the same way. You can be different."

Can't you just hear Matthew disputing this invitation in his own heart? "It's all I've ever known. Other people will never see me the way You see me. Right now, they are sneering and jeering at me. They despise me and judge me and talk about me behind my back. They will never accept me. Don't you understand? You don't know what it's like to be prejudged. You don't know what it's like to grow up in a place like this. You don't know what it's like to be me. The truth is, I deserve a lot of what they say. I've rationalized for so long the way I've lived, but I know deep down inside…well, I can't say it out loud, but I deserve it. I just hate myself, but I know I'm trapped. That's just the way it is. I can't change it. Don't you come here and tell me I can change it. How dare you? *How dare you?*"

Is that what Matthew thought? Makes sense to me. But there's something about Jesus that overcomes all of the venting, self-loathing, doubt, and fear. There's something about Jesus that just listens to our objections and then says, "Come on, it *can* be different."

## The Miracle of Being Valued

Matthew gets up and walks away. He leaves his tax office and follows Jesus. His mind is spinning. His world is shifting. He does not know what it all means yet. He has not calculated yet what the cost will really be. He does not know that he'll never go back to that table. He may think that somehow he'll be scrubbed up, elevated, and honored in a way that he'll be able to still collect taxes, but do so respectably.

I don't know what Matthew thinks, but he knows this: *I'm making a decision, and I will not be the same. I'm making this decision because that man Jesus values me. He makes me feel worthwhile. He respects me even though I know in the deepest part of my being that I have no reason to be valued or respected. But He does!*

Matthew wants his friends to meet Jesus, too, so he quickly organizes a large dinner party. As the party assembles, Jesus has a choice to make. Will He attend? It's one thing for Jesus to walk up and under his own initiative say, "I'm going to choose to talk to you, Matthew." It's quite another to be on the receiving end of an invitation to meet a houseful of Matthews. Would Jesus go? Would He be seen with these people? It's one thing to be seen in public with Matthew on a busy thoroughfare. It's quite another to be invited into Matthew's home where He'd be surrounded by people like him, other people who were also despised.

"Wait a minute, I have a ministry!" Jesus could say. "I have my own reputation to protect. I came here with a certain job to perform. There are certain things that must be done." Jesus might have had all kinds of reasons why He would not sully His own ministry, disparage His own name, and alienate the religious establishment, the Pharisees. "Why, they could be very advantageous to me," He might have argued, "if I'll just keep them on my side." But, no, Jesus is not like that. He is not in relationships based on what the outcomes will be for His benefit. He is one person at a time, one soul at a time, one broken heart at a time. Jesus received and accepted the invitation. In so doing, He extended to Matthew a kind of mercy and grace that Matthew probably had never known before.

I grew up in Seattle in a neighborhood called Ballard. Historically, Ballard has been a Scandinavian enclave. At the beginning of the twentieth century, Scandinavian immigrants found their way to Ballard, which was nestled hard and fast against Shilshole and Salmon Bays, bumping into Puget Sound. Fisherman and timber workers from Scandinavia settled there because the climate and topography were similar to Scandinavia; it felt like home. They created this community named Ballard, which was later subsumed and annexed by the city of Seattle.

As a boy growing up there, it seemed to me that everyone (except me) was of Scandinavian descent. Most people had parents or grandparents who came from the Nordic countries. My friends were named Palmerson or Ericksson or Thorsen or Christiansen. The S-E-Ns were the Norwegians, and the S-O-Ns were the Swedes, and the I-A-Ns were the Danes and the Icelanders. The subtleties of the separate Nordic cultures, so monolithic from the outside, were clearly defined on the inside, in Ballard.

In the fourth grade, we spent the whole school year studying the music of *Finlandia* and the heroic struggle of the Finns battling the Russians for sovereignty, ultimately banishing Russian rule from Finland in 1917. How many of you studied that in the fourth grade? That's just the world in which I grew up; I was happy to be there. I might have fit in to this Nordic enclave, because I had blond hair and blue eyes. But I did not really fit in, because the Scandinavian community was very proud of their heritage, tight knit, and seemed to all gather together in one of the local Lutheran churches, like Ballard First or Phinney Ridge. Our family went to the Church of God near Woodland Park; we were neither Lutheran nor Scandinavian; my mother baked chocolate chip cookies, not Swedish tea cakes. I grew up a part of the Ballard community, but somehow a bit outside of it, too.

When I got to high school, not only did I "suffer" from this I'm-not-a-Scandinavian syndrome, but I also had developed into a consummate geek. I didn't know how to relate to other kids my age because I was kind of backward, socially awkward, and always wanted to be invisible. There was a member of my class, of Swedish descent, who was beautiful, poised, and popular, the kind of girl who'd star in a high school musical. Let's call her Ingrid (changing her name, to protect the innocent). She had a circle of friends that I could never access. Their houses overlooked Puget Sound. They visited Stockholm or Copenhagen for Christmas break. They were the local blue bloods. These kids had the run of Ingraham High School, where I attended.

One day, this gorgeous (and really very sweet) Swedish princess approached me in journalism class and, to my utter and absolute astonishment, spoke to me. She said, "Jim, I'm having a party at my house this Friday night, and I wanted to know if you could come." I was stunned, all but speechless. *She* wanted me to come to a party at *her* house? She couldn't be serious. There must be a God, after all.

I wasn't Jesus being invited to Matthew's house; I was Matthew being invited to Jesus' house. You see, there was no reason in the world for me to be on the invitation list; this smart, savvy, and very attractive young woman did not need any more friends—and she certainly did not need me to be her friend. Her party would be fine without me. It was altogether an extravagant act of generosity, of kindness. That's what it was—a phenomenal gesture of value and respect that transcended my whole adolescent experience. In a way, it was a seminal moment in my entire high school experience.

I'll never forget walking to Ingrid's front door, being welcomed and ushered in, glancing at the crowd of what I considered to be Ingraham's elite on that Friday night. The house was filled with people I knew, but with whom I rarely spoke; we were from wildly different lunchroom tables, if you know what I mean. But the hostess came right over to my side and made me feel quite at home. For a moment, it was so surreal I wondered if I was being set up as the object of a joke, but my apprehension was far from the truth.

Ingrid could not have gained anything from me. But she walked out in the world one day, through the halls of Edward S. Ingraham High School, and she saw me pretending to be okay when I wasn't—and she decided to communicate, unmistakably, you, Jim, are someone worthwhile, worth knowing, worth investing in, worth inviting into my home. Others may pass you by, but I will not. Others may think you invisible, but I do not. You matter.

## A Friend of Outcasts

Our worlds are filled with people like that. You will walk by somebody like me—somebody like Matthew—this week. When you decide whom you will engage in conversation and invite into your life, either you'll be like Jesus or you'll be like most everybody else. I think that Jesus looked into the face of Matthew and saw the truth. Matthew was a soul tortured and a heart broken, and Jesus saw that he could be so much more.

To those who criticized His association with Matthew and his friends, Jesus quoted this divine word from Hosea, "I want you to show love, not offer sacrifices" (Hos 6:6). In other words, I want you to express acts of loving-kindness more than perform acts of worship. I am less interested in your showing up at the temple with your offerings than I am in the way in which you reach out to the person who is brokenhearted. Those who take their cues from this biblical mandate will develop a reputation with the sneering religious establishment, just as Jesus did. They sneered at Him behind His back, calling Him "the friend of sinners" as a kind of pejorative; He transformed it into a badge of honor. God wants us to be friends of sinners.

It's very much like another verse in which the Lord says, "I have told you what to do. What do I require of you except that you do good, that you do what is right, and that you show mercy and kindness and that you walk humbly before Me?" (Mic 6:8, para.). This foundational text is exactly the antithesis of the priorities of the religious leaders of Jesus' day; it escaped them. Something in human nature always draws us into that same pharisaical way of thinking. When are you going to cross the church aisle and speak to somebody you despise? When will Republicans and Democrats see each other's souls instead of their campaign histories? When will we see people cross management and union lines to work for the common good? When will we bridge the different communities of color and ethnicity?

"I know your history," God says, "but I am more interested that you be merciful, that you be kind, that you be gracious. I am more interested in that than anything else." God said that in the Old Testament, but Jesus dusted it off and brought it right into His own day—so should we.

One last thing: if you want to Jesus B. and really become a friend of sinners, you must know who you are, as Jesus did. It's a very, very dangerous game if you yourself are a brooding cauldron of insecurities when you begin associating with those who move in the shadows and live in darkness. If you are uncertain of your own moorings, just keeping company with them can easily draw you into their sad world instead of walking with them into the Lord's light.

You must be secure in the knowledge of who you are—humble in Christ Jesus, but committed to Him—because if you are not absolutely committed to Him, you can find yourself satisfying your own needs under the guise of helping others. This perversion is common. As the Devil prowls about us (and he does), he will tempt us to pose as the crisis manager or problem-solver for others, with mixed motives. That is not what Jesus wants. Jesus was Himself altogether whole, but He only wanted to love other people. They were not reform projects or rescue assignments for Him. Fundamentally, Jesus was the friend of sinners simply because He wanted to be their friend.

As a pastor, I have heard some of the most amazing stories of people's failures. And do you know what I have found? That I loved everybody. I do not mean this in a pretentious way, but when people have shared with me their stories of failure, my heart ached, too. It did not make me judge them. It moved me to say, "Things can get better. God can turn this around. There has got to be a way. This can be healed." I did not start out there, earlier in my ministry, but God has given me the privilege of moving to this place of loving.

The challenge is to do that in our daily walk, not just when people present themselves for help. If we can do this when we are out walking in this world and watching for others, if we can just love them for who they are and what they might be, then we will Jesus B. It's not our job to pummel them with the Gospel or cajole them into the church. It's not our job to show them how wrong they've been and how right we are. We simply need to love them. That's what Jesus did. Jesus B.

# 6. JESUS B. THE STORYTELLER

How would you describe yourself? Could you, in any dimension of your life, imagine yourself saying, "I am like Jesus?" It sounds pretentious and maybe pompous—grandiose beyond our capacity—and yet the Word of God encourages us to Jesus B. in the world today. That's why we're called the body of Christ (1 Cor 12:27). Jesus came and He's coming back, but until then we are the physical and material representation of the person of Christ. We can have the mind of Christ, which means that by the agency of the Holy Spirit, we can actually have our mind transformed so that we can see and interpret the world around us—and respond to it—as Jesus did.

Jesus has left us in this world so that we might Jesus B. until He comes again. We have already identified several things this premise suggests. If you want to Jesus B., you must be baptized. You must allow yourself to be possessed by the Holy Spirit, who can give you victory over the temptation that will surely stalk you as long as you live in this world.

If you would Jesus B., you must walk through this world day by day, calling the best out of other people, helping them to see their potential and their promise, calling them to follow Jesus, as He once called you. If you want to Jesus B., you must decide to be a "friend of sinners" (as the enemies of Jesus branded Him), to befriend people who are outcast. Remember, to be the "friend of sinners," you must be very well grounded, knowing who you are in Christ; otherwise, you may find yourself subsumed into a world that is alien to Christ. If you're going to Jesus B., you have to be able to dine with sinners and publicans. You're going to have to be with tax gatherers and others. You cannot be closeted and cloistered in a Christian community, proud of the fact that you do not really get close to people whom you believe are ethically inferior.

Here's an aspect of your calling that may not be so obvious: If you want to Jesus B., you will have to be a storyteller. That term has not always been a positive label in the English language. Being a *storyteller* has sometimes implied that we fabricate stories to advance our own cause deceitfully. But in its most elemental sense, the word *storyteller* is simply two words joined together to describe someone who *has a story and shares it*. Jesus was the consummate storyteller. He engaged His world—and He communicated truth—by telling stories drawn from everyday life. Have you ever thought about being like Jesus in this way?

## Jesus the Master Storyteller

Matthew 13 is a collection of Jesus' many stories about the kingdom of God. The first is one of the most famous stories ever told by Jesus to describe the nature of the kingdom. What is the kingdom of God like really? It is a difficult concept to grasp. Yet Jesus took this complex and almost ethereal, otherworldly idea and explained it using stories. He took the ordinary things of earthly life and made them emblems of heavenly truth. We see this in the first eight verses:

*Later that same day Jesus left the house and sat beside the lake. A large crowd soon gathered around him, so he got into a boat. Then he sat there and taught as the people stood on the shore. He told many stories in the form of parables such as this one: "Listen! A farmer went out to plant some seeds. As he scattered them across his field, some seeds fell on a footpath, and the birds came and ate them. Other seeds fell on shallow soil with underlying rock. The seeds sprouted quickly because the soil was shallow. But the plants soon wilted under the hot sun, and since they didn't have deep roots, they died. Other seeds fell among thorns that grew up and choked out the tender plants. Still other seeds fell upon fertile soil, and they produced a crop that was thirty, sixty, and even a hundred times as much as had been planted." (vv 1–8)*

Why did Jesus tell so many kinds of stories? Because He was a master teacher, knowing that people would seldom grasp the point if He just delivered abstract ideas. There is a place for what we call didactic teaching, such as the formula that two plus two equals four. You can memorize by rote the fact that two plus two equals four. But if you were to put it into a proverbial story problem (the kind with which all of us have wrestled in a grade school classroom), the equation would make more sense, and its application and significance to everyday life would be cemented in your memory for years.

If I say that two apples and two oranges equal four pieces of fruit, then it has practical application, doesn't it? Mathematics only has value insofar as it translates into something that we can deal with physically—something by which we can interpret and manage our ordinary circumstances or something that gives us knowledge to deal with problems as they arise. Many times people approach spiritual truth as they have mathematics. They suppose it does not matter whether they understand it or not, so long as they memorize a generally accepted expression of it. Its usefulness then, of course, is greatly diminished, because it has no context, no transferable practical purpose.

Jesus modeled a completely different approach to sharing truth. He focused on the integrity of the truth and its transformative power when properly understood and comprehended. Jesus Himself is the truth of God. He is the translation of a heavenly truth into a story that we can understand. It is no surprise then that, as He walked through this world, He shared many moments of great didactic teaching, as in the Sermon on the Mount in Matthew 5. "Blessed are the poor...blessed are they that mourn...blessed are the peacemakers." That is pure didactic teaching. But more people remember the stories of Jesus, and those stories are transformational. Can you think of some?

Luke 15 is a good example. It contains the story of the prodigal son, another story of a woman searching for a lost coin, and still another that tells of a shepherd looking for lost sheep. Have you ever heard Jesus' story of the pearl of great price, in which a merchant gives up everything he has to obtain that one pearl whose value is above all other things? Or have you heard His story of the weeds? Have you heard Jesus' story of the Good Samaritan, in which He speaks of a man left to die by the side of the road by bandits? Subsequently, several devout people passed by and did not help for one reason or another, preoccupied with their own course. However, one man, a man from Samaria (a land disdained by the devout passersby) saw the injured victim and, moved with compassion, stopped to help and sacrificed to be certain that the vulnerable and helpless man was made whole.

These are all stories, aren't they? They are transformational stories. On the previous page, we read the story of a man sowing seed. It is a masterwork, the stuff of genius. Do we want to know what the kingdom of heaven is like? Then Jesus tells us a story. He explains its meaning later (Matt 13:18–23). To paraphrase, He says that the kingdom of heaven is like a man who goes out to throw seed on the ground. The seed falls in several different kinds of soil. Some soil is so hard that roots growing from the seed cannot penetrate it, so the seed bakes in the sun and is gone. Likewise, when the Word of God falls upon stony, indifferent hearts, there is little chance for its survival.

Some seed falls on thin soil, where it takes root, blooms, and grows green for a while, but then weeds, which represent the cares of this world, choke it out. (Jesus specifically refers to the pursuit of wealth.) However, some kingdom truth falls into hearts that are like deep, rich soil. These hearts not only receive the seed, but they also nurture it so that it grows, thrives, and bears fruit. It is magnificent in its straightforward simplicity, an illustration of a foundational truth: the good news of the kingdom of heaven will be dispersed across the world, but it will not always bear fruit—and whether it does bear fruit or not is determined by the soil of the hearts into which it falls.

## Parables from Real Life

Jesus told other stories of eternal significance in this same way—for example, the parable of the talents (an ancient unit of currency, a measure of money). In this narrative, one servant clung to what his master had given him; he held it tight and was afraid to invest, afraid to risk, afraid to take any chances. Others took their chances and invested what had been given to them; the original sums then grew and multiplied, providing healthy returns for the master who owned the talents in the first place. After sharing the story, Jesus declared, "The kingdom of heaven is like that."

He said that the kingdom of heaven is like a man who hires servants and tells them, "Go out and work." Some do, but others do not.

The kingdom of heaven is like a farmer who hires some people in the morning and says, "I'll pay you ten dollars to work today." He goes out at noon and hires more, saying, "I'll pay you ten dollars at the end of the day." Then he hires more people who work only one hour, but he pays them ten dollars, too. One of the earlier hires objects, saying, "Wait a minute! You hired me at the start of the day and you're offering me the same pay that you offered the guy who worked only for an hour? That's not fair!"

But Jesus observed, "The kingdom of heaven does not operate as you think it should. It is God's kingdom; it is altogether His. If He wants to hire this one and pay him ten and He wants to hire you at ten and so on, and if He is faithful to His promise, then what difference does it make how He treats somebody else? You do not determine the equity of heaven. Furthermore, if you serve God for many years and you are welcomed into heaven, but someone else is a wretched criminal to the last dying gasp of breath, when he pleads, 'Lord, I want to go with You to paradise,' what is wrong if the Lord receives him as He receives you? You both deserve to be left at the gate and denied entry. If God wants to be equally gracious to two or ten or all of us, that is His choice." Who made the earlier hire the judge of how and when God extends mercy and shares His wealth?

Jesus excelled at teaching deep truth that makes perfect sense when heard in the context of a story, but truth so deep that it might otherwise be missed or dismissed. Jesus impacted this world and exercises phenomenal influence for the good, in part because of His ability to tell truth with stories that speak into our context and experience, stories that can be remembered with practical application going forward. Is it possible that you could be a storyteller like Jesus? I think so.

## Jesus' Method as Storyteller

What can we learn about Jesus' method of storytelling? First, He paid careful attention to the details of ordinary life. If He was by the seashore of Galilee, He talked about fishing and used that as an illustration. "Follow me and I will make you fishers of men. The kingdom of heaven is like a net that pulls in all kinds of fish and then you have to sort them out. Some are bad, some are good."

When He walked through agricultural regions, He told stories about agriculture. I imagine that if He came to Indiana, where I live, He would give a whole group of stories about the locally familiar, about corn, for instance—how an ear of corn is like this, how growing corn is like that, how a drought is like this, how the soil is like that, how you have to rotate soybeans and corn, and so on. He would be drawing spiritual lessons from the world across the street from my house, from the field upon which I gaze every day.

Jesus drew lessons on the canvas of life, a canvas of the world in which His audience lived. This means you and I have to be able to speak in the language and the culture of our time. We have to be able to draw lessons from the reality of the world around us. Jesus excelled at discussing the details of daily life. He seldom talked about a big sweep of history. He wasn't using the Roman Empire as an illustration of some spiritual truth. He talked about the ordinary, day-to-day routine of ordinary people. He changed the world by doing so.

Second, Jesus found heaven's truth in everything, everywhere. It is not enough to pay attention to the details of daily life; we need to have our eyes opened by the Holy Spirit to allow God to speak to us about what we see. Pray, "Lord, help me to see in the ordinary details of my life today some spiritual lessons, corroborated by Scripture, which can enhance someone else's life—and mine, too."

I remember praying that way on a busy Saturday when my wife and I attended a wedding in our local church. After the ceremony, we hurried to drive many miles to be present for a vocal competition in which our son, Nathanael, was a star (in our estimation, anyway). Nathanael was the featured soloist for his high school's show choir. It was a big deal for him and for us. We raced to the parking lot after the wedding, and I jumped behind the wheel. The roads were icy, our dress clothes were not suited for travel, and I realized I would have to stop to buy gas for the car along the way, which put us even further behind schedule.

As we drove north on the interstate highway, our car began to vibrate in a worsening and inescapable way. I suspected we had a flat tire, and I thought, *I do not have time for this! Nathanael is on stage in just a few minutes.* I began to get angry and spilled the bottle of water from which I was drinking, which made me even more upset. I decided to pull over to check the tires, but there was a snowplow on the road, so I could not easily get to the shoulder. Huge semi-trucks sped by and I thought, *If I stop here I'll be killed just getting out of my car. We'll have to go farther.* I slowed down, limping along, the clock ticking, searching for an exit or safe place to stop.

Then, quite suddenly, there was this still, small voice that said, "Jim, do you want to see a spiritual lesson in real life? Ask Me to help you."

*That's so dumb,* I thought. *You can't heal a flat tire. What are You going to do about it? That's so unrealistic, so stupid.* Impertinent can be my middle name.

Clunk-de-clunk-de-clunk! We finally reached an exit and I slowly moved off the interstate, already visualizing pulling the spare and jack out of the trunk. Frustrated and on edge. I got out of the car. I said, "All right already, Lord, help me. Help me! If You're going to do something about it, come on." I walked around the car, and to my utter astonishment, I could not find any tire flat, low, or even close. I did not know what the problem was—or had been. Everything was as it should be.

I got back in the car and began to drive on, at first tentatively. No clunk-de-clunk now, no unusual vibration or sound at all. No tire was flat. I was perplexed. "Lord, how is it I do not have a flat tire?" I asked. "How can this be?" My native doubt and predisposition denied the obvious. God had intervened. At last I began to accept the reality that defied my reason. "Thank you, Lord, for whatever You did. I do not understand it, but thank You. It has to be You working this out for us, for Nathanael." I sped up and drove the rest of the way, feeling not a single bump, clunk, or vibration. It was smooth. It was like flying, as soon as I acknowledged God for what He had done.

It was real life in this real world with a real lesson from heaven: *Ask Me to help you. And then, say thank You.*

Oh yes, that's my story. And I have told it to you. It is one of many, the tip of the iceberg, so to speak, that describes the power, the goodness, and the intervening grace of God.

Every day is an opportunity for you to learn from your experience, so you can tell a story and Jesus B. to someone else. You can tell true stories that glorify God, stories that help people understand the grace, wonder, and power of God, born out of your own experience. You are then not telling a story you heard from someone else; you are telling your own story. It is the way in which you interpret the world.

It does not necessarily have to be a personal experience. It could be the way in which you just observe nature, as Jesus so often did. It might be your observation of a relationship. Jesus was always comparing our relationship with our Father in heaven to the relationship between a parent and a child. He talks about an unjust judge who is constantly hassled by a woman who wants him to rule in her favor. Finally, the judge says, "All right. I'm tired of your constant whining. Here, I give you what you want." Jesus says that if an unjust judge would do something like that, will not your Father in heaven treat you even better? The answer? Yes, of course. It was Jesus' observation of life around Him, underscoring a spiritual truth.

## The Classroom of Daily Life

Every day is like a classroom in which you can learn about God. Every day you see or experience something that could become a story to share, often a story that comes to an unexpected conclusion. That's what makes it memorable.

Thomas Wheeler was the president of the Massachusetts Life Insurance Company for many years. Wheeler tells a story about driving down a road with his wife somewhere in New England. They pulled off at a gas station in the middle of nowhere, he got out of the car, pumped some gas, and then went into the men's room. He came back to find the gas station attendant, rather scruffy and unkempt, engaged in an animated conversation with his wife beside the car. They were laughing, talking, and just carrying on like old friends. As they drove off, Wheeler said to his wife, "That was quite a conversation you were having with the attendant. It was like you knew him."

"Well, I do know him," she said.

"You know him? How is it that you know him?"

"Truth is, I went to high school with him," she said. "I haven't seen him for years. In fact, he was one of my first loves. We dated for a year or two."

Wheeler looked at her with a sense of satisfaction. "Instead you married me. And I'm the president of Massachusetts Life."

"Tom, you don't get it," his wife said. "If I had married him, he'd be the president of Massachusetts Life and you'd be a gas station attendant."

You'll never forget that story, will you? The whole thing is turned on its head to give you an outcome that you were not expecting. That is good storytelling.

In my life, I've had moments when God opened the horizon of my understanding by illustrating Scripture in the world of experience. When I was twenty years old, my parents said, "We'd like to send you to Europe." My cousins, John and Tim, are like brothers to me. I was raised as an only child, and my cousin John is a year older than me, Tim is just a bit younger, and I am in the middle. These two young men were going to Europe for six weeks to see the Munich Olympic Games and tour around the continent and United Kingdom. I thought that was a great idea, but I was stunned when my parents said, "We want you to go with them." I protested that I did not have the money, that there was no way I could afford the adventure. I was a sophomore in college; there were enough expenditures lined up for the year ahead without this extravagant one.

But they said, "No, no. We want to pay for it. We want to fully underwrite the cost."

"I cannot accept that from you," I persisted. "You're my mom and dad. You've done everything for me. You work hard. Buy a new refrigerator, Mom, not a plane ticket for me. Dad, you could use a new car yourself. That old Chevy II you're still driving—I can't believe you're driving it. Do something else with your cash."

My mom looked straight at me and she said, "You know what? I've never been to Europe, and I probably will never go. You won't be able to understand this until you have children, but you're our son. In a way you can't comprehend, our lives are made complete by the way in which you will experience life. We will have joy knowing that you're at the foot of the Eiffel Tower. We will be exhilarated to think that you're looking at Big Ben. When you go to the Coliseum at Rome, when you see the Olympic Games open in Munich, when you drive through Salzburg and see where Mozart lived and wrote his music, when you're in the Alps of France, and when you tour Belgium, in all of that we will be blessed and made better because you experienced it."

I just looked at them and thought, *You are out of your minds.*

Now I have sons of my own. My wife and I work hard, and do you know what? It's all about our boys. When they get to go places and do things that I never will, my own life is made more complete. When I saw this with my own children, I learned that God has pleasure when I am filled with joy. There was a day when I could not receive things from God because I did not feel worthy of them. I would not allow myself to have pure, unbridled joy about something just because I enjoyed it. All of a sudden, it all came back to me; these relationships in life became a parable of my relationship to God. God is glad for me to laugh. He is glad for me to enjoy. He is glad for me to have special moments. He finds pleasure in it.

If something is righteous, if it is a gift from Him, if it is within His boundaries, I should accept it without reservation. How transformational that was in my life! Instead of saying, "No, no, I will not accept that, I cannot," I've learned how to say, "Thank You, Lord."

*That's my story. And I have shared it with you. And, yes, it's still just the tip of the iceberg, just one of many stories to tell about the goodness and calling of God.*

What's your story? What's that, you say? You do not believe you have one or two or any to tell? You have not seen God at work in your world? You cannot recall a moment when the Lord intervened, even supernaturally, on your road of life—or anyone else's? You have never been invited by God to receive a gift, undeserved? You have never sensed His protection or provision? You have never seen His hand in the creation around you? You have observed no lesson that honors Him in circumstance or nature?

Ask the Lord to teach you lessons every day through your own experience and the world you see, so that you can tell those stories for the glory of God, declaring the truth of God. Ask God to make you a storyteller. For Jesus' sake. And then, open your eyes and ears and be willing to speak. *Jesus B.*

# 7. PEOPLE WILL PRAISE YOU
## —SOMETIMES!

If you would Jesus B., you can expect to be both praised and condemned. We get a glimpse of this truth in Matthew 21, the story of our Lord's last entry into Jerusalem:

*Most of the crowd spread their garments on the road ahead of him, and others cut branches from the trees and spread them on the road. Jesus was in the center of the procession, and the people all around him were shouting, "Praise God for the Son of David! Blessed is the one who comes in the name of the Lord! Praise God in highest heaven!" The entire city of Jerusalem was in an uproar as he entered. "Who is this?" they asked. And the crowds replied, "It is Jesus, the prophet from Nazareth in Galilee." (vv 8–11)*

In Matthew 27, we find Jesus apprehended, arrested, and on trial before Pilate, the Roman governor. Pilate is the most powerful authority in the land, the agent of the Emperor. Notice what happens when Jesus stands before him:

*Meanwhile, the leading priests and the elders persuaded the crowd to ask for Barabbas to be released and for Jesus to be put to death. So the governor asked again, "Which of these two do you want me to release to you?" And the crowd shouted back, "Barabbas!" Pilate responded, "Then what should I do with Jesus, who is called the Messiah?" They shouted back, "Crucify him!" "Why?" Pilate demanded. "What crime has he committed?" But the mob roared even louder. "Crucify him!" (vv 20–23)*

How can it be? How could Jesus' situation change so dramatically in less than a week? The pivotal factor in these two passages from Matthew's Gospel is the crowd. Here we see Jesus and the mass of humanity, and we realize that the people who celebrated His arrival on one day could suddenly turn on Him the next. The crowd praises Jesus then condemns Him. So it is for anyone who would Jesus B.

As Jesus entered Jerusalem for the Passover, He fulfilled two ancient prophecies of the Old Testament. Isaiah 62 and Zechariah 9 both foretold how the King of God's people would come riding on a donkey's colt, to the approval and praise of the entire city. And so it was. As this great Jewish holiday and festival approached, they gathered in the holy city of Jerusalem to celebrate. Then Jesus arrived. He came first to a little village called Bethany on the far side of the Mount of Olives, which overlooks Jerusalem. Scripture tells us that Jesus instructed His disciples to go into Jerusalem, where they would find a donkey and a colt, which they were to bring back to him. They did so, placing their garments on the donkey's back so that Jesus could ride it into town, following the winding road from the Mount of Olives that descended into the valley of the Brook Kidron, and then back up into the city of Jerusalem itself toward Mount Zion.

As Jesus entered the city, the crowd went wild. Why, it made a rally for a victorious politician or a championship sports team look lame. Everyone seemed to ask, "Who is this? Who is this?" Those who were not along the parade route, hearing the noise and commotion, must have said, "What's going on? What's going on?" And the crowd cried back, "It's Jesus! It's Jesus, the One from Nazareth. Blessed is He Who comes in the name of the Lord!"

## Why People Loved Jesus

As He came into town, they cried out the word, *Hosanna.* It literally meant, "Save us!" It was not just a plea for mercy, but a shout of confidence. "You there, we praise *You!* Save us, save us! We know *You* can. Do it now!" Why did they say this? What moved them to praise Jesus? As we read about this event in the four Gospels, we see various angles and details.

Mark 11 says they were spellbound by His teaching. He spoke with such authority. He spoke so convincingly. He was so persuasive, inspiring, and hopeful. He helped make sense out of the tangled web of their difficult and trying world. In the chaotic ordinary, He gave them a sense of heaven. The crowd loved Him for this. They were drawn to the words that came out of His mouth. That's why they embraced Him.

Mark tells us another reason that people loved Him: He had high regard for John the Baptist. John had earlier been murdered by the Roman puppet king, Herod, in the northern region of Galilee. When Herod put John to death, the people were deeply grieved because they believed he had been a prophet of God. Likewise, Jesus spoke boldly, honestly, and authentically about the evils of their day. Jesus spoke without fear about John the Baptist. He explained that John the Baptist was about whom Isaiah prophesied in the Old Testament, *the voice calling in the wilderness.*

John was an extraordinary man of God; by Jesus' testimony, no one who had walked the earth before was greater than he. The crowd admired and was drawn to Jesus' courageous proc-lamation and affirmation of John the Baptist, who had been murdered by the government. When the government believes someone is a troublemaker and removes that person from the scene, it takes some courage to stand up and say, "Wait a minute, wait a minute...that was a great voice." Yet Jesus would not be cowed by those political forces, and the crowd loved Him for it.

In other Gospels, we read that because Jesus was a wonder-worker, crowds followed Him to see the miracles that He did. He was forever healing and making people whole. We might call this His *work of blessing*. Whether bodies or relationships were broken, people were burdened with heavy stones of guilt and shame, or people were afraid of their circumstances, Jesus was always about lifting the load, making things right, healing injuries, and helping people see a new day. This work of blessing drew a crowd. How could they help but praise Him?

Yet some who shouted "Hosanna" to welcome Jesus into Jerusalem on that first Palm Sunday were in the courtyard of Pilate's palace later in the week, demanding that Jesus be crucified. It is very possible that most of the city, which was so swept up in the receiving of Jesus, was also swept up in the judgment and condemnation of Jesus. We do not know with certainty who lined the parade route and who crowded before the balcony of Pilate. Yet, it is clear there were masses of people at both ends of this Holy Week story, praising and condemning Jesus.

## Why People Turned on Jesus

Why would a crowd so positive about Jesus on Palm Sunday shrink from view and then turn to condemn Him the following Friday? Scripture tells us that key voices in the crowd spoke against Jesus and persuaded the people to turn against Him. That's the problem with crowds: They are fickle. They can praise you now and condemn you later. You live on an emotional roller coaster when a crowd begins to follow you.

I doubt that the voices inciting these crowds stood on a platform to make their appeal. They did not shout, "You fools! Why are you following Jesus? Don't you know that He is usurping Caesar? Don't you know that He's going to bring the Roman army down on us? Don't you know we're all going to suffer for it?" No, they did not have to take a prominent, public role by the full light of day. They only needed to begin whispering doubt in the background.

You know how such voices do their work—in quiet, genteel conversation that undermines the reputation of someone else when that person is not present. Such voices sap the energy of a group and tear it down instead of building it up. I believe that is what the Scripture describes here. People in authority, respectable people, influential people, sowed doubt in the crowd. I can hear them say, "Wait a minute, don't be so quick to release Jesus. Be careful. Be careful. There's a wild move afoot, and we don't know what the price is going to be." Suspicion and cynicism began to prevail, and the crowd was drawn away from hope back into fear. It began to lose its own better judgment.

That is how crowd mentality works. It can accomplish much good or much evil. Groupthink and panic can submerge and subdue our thoughtfulness and objectivity.

Beyond all the power of a group dynamic, I think Jesus Himself was a critical factor in the crowd's turn of sentiment. He did not meet the crowd's expectations. They wanted somebody who would do things on their terms, their way. Much anger and conflict in this world are consequences of people's expectations not being met. We may generate expectations inside of ourselves and impose them on someone else without their will or consent; then, when expectations so generated are not met, anger ensues.

The expectations that the crowds of Jerusalem placed on Jesus were not the expectations that God had placed on Jesus.

They had followed Him so far, but realized He was not the person that they thought He was. He did not raise up an army. He did not deliver them from political and economic oppression. He said He ruled a different kind of a kingdom, not the nation-state for which they were looking. He called them to a different way of life, not one that was fed by their own petty jealousies and greed. In the end, this became crystal clear. This man they had acclaimed suddenly had been arrested and was now in prison—but He was not breaking out. He was not striking all the Roman soldiers dead, and He was not cursing in the face of Pilate. He just stood there, broken, manacled, beaten, and humiliated. The crowd that had run toward the star celebrity now ran away from Him, because His cause seemed to be lost.

So it is in life. We do not always meet other people's expectations. What then? Jesus B. And how is it possible that we could be like Jesus in such a world? In the preceding chapters, I have made the case that we, by our conduct and motivated by a will formed by God's Holy Spirit in us, can actually be the body of Christ. We can be Jesus, here and now. And that requires several things. We must:

1.  Step forward and be publicly baptized. This declares your commitment to serve God as a citizen of His kingdom.

2.  Be filled by the Holy Spirit. The Spirit within will enable you to overcome all the temptations this world can throw.

3.  Be God's light in a dark world. Call the best out of other people and show them how they can bear God's light and life to those who need Him.

4.  Be a healer. Speak strength, wholeness, and recovery into the lives of broken people and a broken world.

5.  Be a friend of sinners. Reach out to those who are despised and unwelcome in the rest of society, those

who struggle with guilt and shame, those without hope and heaven's frame; help them see their supreme worth in the sight of God.

6. Be a storyteller. Relate your experiences of daily life with God in ways that can be remembered and understood.

## How to Receive Praise and Judgment

If you will Jesus B. in all of these ways, I promise that you will be praised. Never seek praise; there's no evidence that Jesus ever did. He did not act or speak as He did to win the favor of anyone. He did it because He loved others and to fulfill the will of God.

We must learn how to receive praise; some people crave other people's acknowledgement or affirmation, but such thirst must never define the why of what we do. I spent a lot of my life not being able to receive praise, always turning it away and saying, "Well, I don't deserve that." I could not be authentic; I became artificial in the receiving of praise.

Jesus was altogether authentic. He received the praise of people without pretense. When you and I are being Jesus in the world, people will praise what we do, and we need to be able to say thank you. Just say thank you. "The Lord is good, thank you so much." "The Lord is so gracious, thanks for seeing that." "Thanks for saying that." "Thanks for that word of encouragement." We need to learn to receive praise as Jesus did, in the sense that we are humble, but honest, in receiving it—and then turn it back toward heaven. "Thank you" is sometimes the hardest thing to say sincerely, but it is the best thing to say when you are being affirmed.

By the same token, if you will Jesus B., you will have to learn how to receive condemnation and judgment. That is also a very difficult lesson to learn. It is hard to receive criticism with grace, instead of bitterness and without a sense of self-righteous defense or trying to prove that you are the one in the right. It is hard to Jesus B. when people who once were for you seem to now be against you. It is tough when someone who was once a close friend seems now to pass you by without even acknowledging you. It is a challenge to Jesus B. when you know that something is wrong in a relationship and cannot imagine why, yet you need to graciously not lose your footing and lash out.

As Jesus endured the harsh judgment of the crowd in the days and hours before the cross, He remarkably held His tongue. So much might He have said! But no, His words were few and measured. Silence was His stance, in the main. Jesus was always ready to defend others, to stand for the weak and vulnerable, but He was quiet in the face of His own tormentors. Self-restraint is often the best self-defense.

And, of course, Jesus famously faced those who condemned Him with mercy. "Father forgive them, for they know not what they do" is, perhaps, the most famous word from the cross. It captures powerfully the Lord's grace, focus, remedy, and power. Loving those who are our enemies is the way of Jesus; it is the way of overcoming cruel and unjust judgment.

Finally, coping with the rejection of others requires us to know exactly who we are. Jesus fully understood Who He was, why He was here, and what He had to do. His cues were heaven-sent, not originating in this desperate world. John's Gospel reminds us: "Jesus knew that the Father had given him authority over everything and that he had come from God and would return to God" (John 13:3). He knew exactly where He came from and where He was going. This empowered Him to endure and then triumph with grace, sure-footed and brave, and without bitterness or hate. We can, too.

Jesus challenged the *status quo*. He clearly was a threat to people who liked things in certain ways—their own ways. He did not strive to meet the expectations of others, only the expectations of God. As a result, popular opinion blew hot and cold. We need to receive praise or judgment as Jesus did, trusting God.

We may want all of our days to be Palm Sundays instead of Good Fridays, but if we're going to Jesus B., we will have some of both. Nevertheless, we never need to lose our confidence and faith in the One who has called us, sent us, and promised us.

*Jesus B.* Find life. And change the world.

CPSIA information can be obtained
at www.ICGtesting.com
Printed in the USA
FFOW05n1009210616

9 781593 176808